FROM THE LIBRARY OF
BERKELEY COLLEGE

New York:
NYC (Midtown and Lower Manhattan)
Brooklyn • White Plains

New Jersey:
Newark • Paramus • Woodbridge
Woodland Park

Berkeley College Online:
BerkeleyCollege.edu/Online

Berkeley College®

Praise for *Selling with Noble Purpose*

"Lisa McLeod is an expert in sales leadership. McLeod has coached top tier sales teams at Apple, Kimberly-Clark, and Procter & Gamble, where we both began our careers. She knows what it takes to drive growth."

—Jim Stengel
Former Chief Global Marketing Officer,
Procter & Gamble; Author, *Grow*

"A must-read manifesto for anyone who is serious about sales leadership."

—Joseph Grenny
Author, *Crucial Conversations*

"McLeod has coached sales leaders at Apple, Kimberly-Clark, Pfizer, and other top organizations. She combines a wealth of field experience with unique insights to drive revenue."

—Marshall Goldsmith
#1 Leadership Thinker in the World (Thinkers50 –
Harvard Business Review)

"Lisa McLeod knows what is at the core of great sales leadership and communicates this simply to help people reshape their mindset and drive better results. I recommend her work to any leader who wants to align their sales force toward a higher purpose, get closer to clients, and drive more revenue."

—Michel Koopman
CEO getAbstract

"If you sell based on a deep mission and purpose, revenue will follow. As Lisa Earle McLeod explains in this remarkable book, you have to start with how to change another life . . . then work back from that purpose."

—Tom Rath
Author, *Strengths-Finder*

"Lisa McLeod, who has worked with salespeople for 25 years, has written a sales book with the power to rouse and transform. If you sell for a living, *Selling with Noble Purpose* is a shot of adrenaline that can get you to re-imagine your world and career in ways you might not have thought possible."

—Mark Levy
Founder of the marketing firm, Levy Innovation

"NSP does for sales what *Man's Search for Meaning* did for psychology. This book shows that if you find your purpose, selling becomes effortless."

—Stephen Shapiro
Author, *Best Practices are Stupid*

Great sales professionals focus on worth to their prospects, not on wealth to their own pockets. They compassionately sell with soul, rather than cleverly influencing with style. *Selling with Noble Purpose* will touch your life, transform your approach, and guarantee the long-term loyalty of your customers.

—**Chip R. Bell**
Author, *Wired and Dangerous*

"Professional selling has been around long enough so there should not be any more 'secrets.' But, apparently, there are. In this absolute masterpiece of a work, Lisa Earle McLeod reveals this secret and shares the key that opens the door to helping you provide more value to people's lives and a huge increase in your income. Follow Ms. McLeod's teachings and—not only will you be hugely more financially successful—you'll LOVE what you're doing even more! (And, if you're a sales manager, this book is one of those you'll not only want all your sales team to read, but you'll most likely want to make a team study of it. It's that good!)"

—**Bob Burb**
Author, *The Go Giver* and *Endless Referrals*

selling
with
noble
purpose

selling *with* noble purpose

How to
Drive Revenue *and* Do Work That Makes You Proud

Lisa Earle McLeod

WILEY

John Wiley & Sons, Inc.

Published by John Wiley & Sons, Inc., Hoboken, New Jersey.
Published simultaneously in Canada.

For general information about our other products and services, please contact our Customer Care Department within the United States at (800) 762-2974, outside the United States at (317) 572-3993 or fax (317) 572-4002.

Wiley publishes in a variety of print and electronic formats and by print-on-demand. Some material included with standard print versions of this book may not be included in e-books or in print-on-demand. If this book refers to media such as a CD or DVD that is not included in the version you purchased, you may download this material at http://booksupport.wiley.com. For more information about Wiley products, visit www.wiley.com.

Library of Congress Cataloging-in-Publication Data:

McLeod, Lisa, 1963-
    Selling with noble purpose: how to drive revenue and do work that makes you proud/Lisa McLeod.
        Includes index.
        ISBN: 978-1-118-40809-4 (cloth)
        ISBN: 978-1-118-42185-7 (ebk)
        ISBN: 978-1-118-41766-9 (ebk)
        ISBN: 978-1-118-43443-7 (ebk)
            1. Selling. I. Title.
    HF5438.25
    658.85—dc23

2012032656

Printed in the United States of America

10 9 8 7 6 5 4 3 2 1

For my dad,
Jay Earle,
a man who made a difference
at work and home

Contents

Introduction

What Is Selling with Noble Purpose?

Hearts are the strongest when they beat in response to noble ideals.
—Ralph Bunche
Winner of the 1950 Nobel Peace Prize

The words *selling* and *noble* are rarely seen together. Most people believe that money is the primary motivator for top salespeople and that doing good by the world runs a distant second. That belief is wrong.

Six years ago, I was part of a consulting team that was asked by a major biotech firm to conduct a six-month-long double-blind study of its sales force. The purpose of the study was to determine what behaviors separated top salespeople from the average ones. The study revealed something no one expected: the top performers all had far more pronounced *sense of purpose* than their average counterparts.

The salespeople who sold with noble purpose—who truly wanted to make a difference to customers—consistently outsold the salespeople who were focused on sales goals and money.

It was a startling discovery that I might have missed had it not been for a curbside conversation at the Phoenix airport.

I was finishing a two-day ride along with a sales rep. As she dropped me off at the airport, I asked her a question I hadn't asked the other reps: "What do you think about when you go on sales calls? What's going on in your head?"

"I don't tell this to many people," she confessed, looking around the car as though someone was going to hear her secret. "When I go on sales calls, I always think about this particular patient who came up to me one day during a call on a doctor's office."

"I was standing in the hallway talking to one of the doctors. I was wearing my company name badge, so I stood out. All of a sudden this elderly woman taps me on the shoulder."

"'Excuse me, Miss,' she said. 'Are you from the company that makes drug x?'"

"'Yes, ma'am.'"

"'I just want to thank you,' she said. 'Before my doctor prescribed your drug, I barely had enough energy to leave the house. But now I can visit my grandkids; I can get down on the floor to play with them. I can travel. So thank you. You gave me back my life.'"

The sales rep told me, "I think about that woman every day. If it's 4:30 on a rainy Friday afternoon, other sales reps go home. I don't. I make the extra sales call because I know I'm not just pitching a product. I'm saving people's lives. That grandmother is my higher purpose."

Sitting in that blistering Phoenix heat, I realized she had said something incredibly important. I thought about that conversation during the entire flight back to Atlanta.

Our consulting team had spent months shadowing salespeople all over the country. We'd conducted in-depth interviews and analyzed every aspect of the sales calls. But this was the first time anyone had spoken so openly and dramatically about their mindset.

Was the big differentiator between top performers and average performers really a sense of purpose?

I went back to the transcripts of the interviews looking for purpose, and I didn't see it at first. But then I looked closer—and there it was, in the rep who said, "My dad was a doctor. Doctors have an even harder job than most people realize. I want to make it easier for them." It was there in the rep who was thrilled to be discussing the science, practically glowing when he said, "Isn't it amazing the way that we're able to do these things?" There were other reps who talked about the impact they had on nurses and patients. And although none of these people actually used the word *purpose*, it was there.

At the end of the project, the client asked us to look across all the reps and identify who we thought were the top performers. It was a double-blind study, so the other consultants and I didn't know who was at the top and who was just average.

I found seven reps who had that sense of purpose when reviewing the interviews. I told the client, "I think these seven are top-performing salespeople."

I was 100 percent right, which confirmed my belief: top performers weren't driven solely by money. They were driven by purpose.

And the rep in Phoenix who went on sales calls thinking about the grandmother? She was the number one salesperson in the country three years running. While her average counterparts were trying to win the incentive trip, she was playing for much higher stakes, which translated into higher sales.

Ironic, isn't it? The salespeople who cared about something more than just money wound up selling *more* than the salespeople who were focused only on quota. This surprising finding led me on a quest to understand what goes on inside the minds of top-performing salespeople and how leaders can replicate that mindset throughout their organization. After six years of research and 10,000 hours of studying salespeople, the results leave no doubt: a Noble Sales Purpose (NSP) is the difference between a merely effective sales force and one that's truly outstanding.

You don't need to look any further than the auto industry to see what happens when salespeople lack a Noble Sales Purpose.

The auto industry has genius engineers. They do extensive consumer research to identify exactly what we might want or need in a car. Their marketing people create compelling ads. But what happens when you go to the dealership? The only thing the salesperson wants to know is, "How much a month can you pay?" and, "Do you have good credit?" Years of work, thousands of hours researching the consumer, millions of dollars spent, and it all falls apart on the showroom floor.

As anyone who has done it can attest, buying a car can be an absolutely soul-sucking experience. Car salespeople don't care about making a difference in your life. All they care about is closing the deal—because closing the deal is the *only thing their sales manager has told them to care about.*

The conversations managers have with salespeople drive the conversation salespeople have with customers. The internal conversation becomes the external conversation. So if the internal conversations are only about price, volume, and targets, with no mention of a larger purpose, that's exactly what your salespeople will discuss with customers.

Lest you have any doubt about the power of purpose, consider this: the data from a 10-year growth study of more than 50,000 brands around the world show that companies who put improving people's lives at the center of all they do outperform the market by a huge margin.[1] The study, done by an independent consulting group in partnership with former Procter & Gamble chief marketing officer (CMO) Jim Stengel, revealed that "those who center their business on improving people's lives have a growth rate triple that of their competitors, and they outperform the market by a huge margin."

Jim Collins and Jerry Porras of *Built to Last* fame also documented that organizations driven by purpose and values outperformed the market by 15:1—and outperformed comparison companies by 6:1

The research is clear, and it confirms what we know in our hearts to be true: a noble purpose engages people's passion in a way that spreadsheets don't.

You don't have to create world peace. Your noble sales purpose can be about making your customers more successful or about changing your industry.

A friend of mine in politics has worked in several congressional and Senate offices and on some large national campaigns. She once told me, "In every office, there's always a TB."

"What's a TB?" I asked her.

"A true believer," she said. "That starry-eyed optimist who still believes they can make difference. But here's the thing all the jaded staffers don't tell you—everyone else in the office is secretly jealous of the true believer."

---

[1]Millward Brown Optimor, "Stengel Study of Business Growth."

I've come to understand the reason everyone is jealous of the true believer: we all have a secret true believer inside of us, just waiting for permission to come out.

Selling with Noble Purpose is about igniting the true believer that lurks in the heart of every salesperson. Because as much as salespeople want to make money, they also want to make a difference.

PART

I

Why Noble Sales Purpose Matters and Where to Find Yours

In the end, it is impossible to have a great life unless it is a meaningful life. And it is very difficult to have a meaningful life without meaningful work.

—Jim Collins, *Good to Great*

Making a difference and making a living are not incompatible goals. As a sales leader, you can pursue both. If you want to be truly successful, you *must* pursue both.

Unfortunately, the current sales narrative of your business is very likely flawed, fatally out of sync with what really matters to salespeople and customers. As you'll discover in *Selling with Noble Purpose*, there's a widespread, unspoken problem in sales. It's the startling gap between what organizations want salespeople to do when they're with customers versus what most organizations *really* reinforce on a daily basis. But it doesn't have to be this way.

In Part I of *Selling with Noble Purpose*, you'll learn how a Noble Sales Purpose (NSP) reframes the sales narrative of your organization in a way that helps you drive revenue *and* do work that makes you proud. We'll explore what an NSP is and what it's not—and why it matters to you and your sales force.

We'll look at how overemphasis on profit and sales quotas has eroded customer trust and sales force morale. We'll also explore the brain science behind NSP and how it taps into two universal human needs: connection and meaning.

We'll look at how a variety of organizations have used NSP to drive revenue and improve morale. At the end of Part I, we'll walk through the process of creating your own NSP.

Your NSP will become your North Star—a tool to reset yourself during times of challenge and a methodology to take your team to higher levels of performance.

1

The Great Sales Disconnect

Suppose that you wrote the following goal on your office whiteboard: "I want to make as much money as possible." Now suppose your clients saw it. How would they feel? How would you feel knowing that they'd seen it? Would you feel proud or embarrassed?

What if you went over your prospect list, and the only thing written next to each prospect's name was a dollar figure and a projected close date? Would your prospects be happy if they saw that? Would they want to do business with you?

Probably not; it reduces them to nothing more than a number. Yet, that's exactly how most organizations talk about their customers on a daily basis.

Think about the typical conversation a sales manager has with his or her sales rep. It usually goes something like this:

"When are you going to close this? How much revenue will it be? Are all the key decision makers involved? Who's the competition? What do you need to close this deal?"

All of the questions are about *when and how* we're going to collect revenue from the customer. Very few managers ask about the impact the sale will have on the customer's business or life.

This is a big problem.

Imagine a salesperson walking into a customer's office and opening the sales call by plopping a revenue forecast down on the customer's desk, announcing, "I have you projected for $50,000 this month. Give me an order now!"

That rep would be thrown out in a second. Yet that's the kind of language most organizations use when they talk about their customers internally. It's like two different worlds.

We expect salespeople to focus on customers' needs and goals when they're in front of customers, but the majority of our internal conversations are about our own revenue quotas. Although it's an unintended disconnect, it's a fatal one.

Most organizations want to have a positive impact on their customers' lives. It makes good business sense, and it appeals to our more noble instincts. Yet when managers are caught up inside the pressure cooker of daily business, their desire to improve the customer's life is eclipsed by quotas, quarterly numbers, and daily sales reports.

This results in salespeople who don't have any sense of a higher purpose, other than "making the numbers." It sounds good in theory, but customers can tell the difference between the salespeople who care about them and those who care only about their bonuses.

The great disconnect between what we want salespeople to do when they're in the field (focus on the customer) versus what we emphasize and reinforce internally (our own targets and quotas) results in mediocre sales performance.

What Lack of Purpose Costs a Sales Force

When the customer becomes nothing more than a number to you, you become nothing more than a number to the customer—and your entire organization suffers. When you overemphasize financial goals at the expense of how you make a difference to customers, you make it extremely difficult for your salespeople to differentiate themselves from the competition.

And the problem doesn't stop there. It has a ripple effect on salespeople, who:

- Start thinking only about the short term.
- Fail to understand the customer's environment.
- Cannot connect the dots between your products and customers' goals.
- Cannot gain access to senior levels within the customer.

Then the problem escalates:

- Customers view you as a commodity.
- You have little or no collaboration with them.
- Customers place undue emphasis on minor problems.
- Customer churn increases.
- Contracts are constantly in jeopardy over small dollar amounts.
- Salespeople's default response is to lower the price.
- Sales has a negative perception in the rest of the organization.
- There is little or no product innovation.
- Sales force turnover increases.
- Salespeople try to game the comp plan.
- Top performers become mid-level performers.
- Salespeople view their fellow salespeople as the competition.
- Sales force morale declines.

It's not a pretty picture. When the internal conversation is all about money, the external conversation becomes all about money. And all of a sudden, that's the last thing you're making.

Companies have tried a variety of methods to solve this problem. Organizations spend millions on sales training programs that teach salespeople how to ask better questions and engage the customers. They spend even more millions on customer relationship management (CRM) systems to capture critical customer information. They host off-site retreats to create mission and vision statements. They hire expensive consultants to craft their value story.

But the results are short lived at best. Salespeople abandon the training. No one updates the CRM. The mission and vision are put on a meaningless placard in the lobby. And the value story is reduced to a bunch of ho-hum slides that sound just like everyone else's.

The reason these solutions don't deliver sustained improvement is because they address only the symptoms. They don't tackle the root cause: the lack of purpose.

Peter Drucker, widely considered the most influential management thinker in the second half of the twentieth century, once famously said, "Profit is not the purpose of a business but rather the test of its validity."

I'll take that a step further: *driving revenue is not the purpose of a sales force; it's the test of its effectiveness.*

When targets and quotas become the primary organizing element of your business, the result is mediocrity at best. Although profit is of course critical, it's not the best starting point for driving sales revenue. To do that, you have to start with a Noble Sales Purpose (NSP).

An NSP is a definitive statement about how you make a difference in the lives of your customers. It speaks to why you're in business in the first place. Used correctly, your NSP drives every decision you make and every action you take. It becomes the underpinning for all your sales activities.

One of my clients is a provider of information technology (IT) services for small businesses. Their NSP is simply, "We help small businesses be more successful." It drives everything they do. Every decision, large or small, must pass through that filter, "Will this help us make small businesses more successful?" If the answer is no, they don't do it. Every new product and service they create—every sales call they're on—is focused on how they can make their customers' businesses more successful.

Since implementing their NSP strategy, their sales are up 35 percent. In a tough economy when customers are cutting back on outside IT services, their business is growing.

An NSP is a new way to think about your business. Doing business from an NSP perspective is counter to the way most corporations, entrepreneurs, and salespeople have been told to think—and that's exactly why it works.

Instead of making profit your sole purpose, you emphasize the impact you have on customers. Profits are the result of your work, not the sole purpose of your efforts. It might sound like heresy, but purpose is the secret to driving *more* revenue.

Ad agency owner Roy Spence, who works with Southwest Airlines and Walmart, says, "Purpose is your reason for being; [it] goes beyond making money and it almost always results in making more money than you ever thought possible."

An NSP drives more revenue than financial goals alone because an NSP taps into a human instinct even more powerful than our desire for money.

Why NSP Makes You Money

In his book *Drive: The Surprising Secret about What Motivates Us*, author Daniel Pink—who has written extensively on the changing world of work—debunks the myth of the carrot and the stick as effective motivators. He writes, "The science shows that the secret to high performance isn't our biological drive or our reward-and-punishment drive, but our third drive—our deep-seated desire to direct our own lives, to expand and extend our abilities, and to live a life of purpose." Pink goes on to say, "Humans, by their nature, seek purpose—a cause greater and more enduring than themselves."

Pink's research reveals the discord between what social science knows (humans crave purpose) and business does (the carrot and stick). Nowhere is this dissension greater than in sales, where organizations continue to dangle incentive programs, bonuses, and trips in front of salespeople, hoping that it will motivate them. Yet time and again, the incentive programs produce short-terms spikes in performance from a small percentage of people. In most organizations, the top performers remain the same year after year, while the rest of the sales force stays stuck in the mediocre middle.

What's missing is a sense of larger purpose.

When you ask salespeople who are performing at an average level why they go to work, very few will give you an answer that sounds anything remotely like a sense of purpose. They usually just talk about money. But when you ask top-performing salespeople why they go to work, they will almost always talk about having a larger noble purpose.

Here's the disconnect: top performers are driven by purpose, but their company leadership almost never discusses any purpose beyond making money.

The very thing that differentiates top performers—a sense of purpose—is almost never mentioned by company leadership.

What's ironic is that many companies *do* make a difference to their customers and serve a larger purpose. They just don't talk about it with the salespeople.

I once worked with a health care products company that was literally saving people's lives. The senior leaders made a regular practice of describing the meaningful impact their products had on customers to the manufacturing team, the customer service group, and even the accountants. Yet it was like they developed a sudden case of amnesia when they interacted with the sales department. All the discussions in sales meetings and coaching sessions were about quotas and revenue or products' features and rollout plans. They almost never talked about the impact the products had on *actual human beings*.

It was as if they believed that their sales force was some bizarre strange animal, living in a parallel universe where meaning, purpose, and contribution were irrelevant. When it came to sales, it was only about the money.

Of course, this was huge mistake.

The very people who should be on fire for making the difference to the customers—the sales force—almost never heard it mentioned. Talk about a mismatch.

Is it any wonder that their sales force struggled to maintain margins and was often treated like a commodity by their customers? If all you talk about is money and margin when you're inside the organization, it's only natural that's where things go in customer conversations. What else are your salespeople going to discuss?

Is it any surprise they had high turnover in sales and their best people left for a competitor? The salespeople felt very little affiliation for their company, the leadership, or even the products. It was never about anything but numbers, so when another company started offering the reps a better comp plan, they jumped at it.

If your sales force isn't passionate about the impact your company has on customers, they don't have a strong sense of affiliation with your organization. They're not able to differentiate you from your competitors in front of the customers. Their work becomes just a job—one that they'll leave for something better at the drop of a hat.

That's why you need an NSP—it solves the great sales disconnect. It combines making money with making a difference, and it bridges the gap between internal conversation and external conversation.

What's Gained from Approaching Sales with NSP

Your NSP points you in a nobler and, ultimately, more profitable direction. It's the starting point for a series of changes that can dramatically improve your sales force and the bottom line.

An NSP:

- Brings the customer voice to the front and center of the conversation.
- Keeps your sales force focused on quotas *and* customers.
- Provides an organizing framework for planning and decision making.
- Reinforces the right sales behavior.

- Improves the quality of your existing sales training.
- Helps mid-level performers set more challenging goals.
- Helps top performers stay focused.
- Acts as a reset button during times of challenge and change.

This book is written for sales leaders, because you are the ones who set the tone for your organization. Whether you're a vice president of sales, a sales manager, or an aspiring sales leader, you have the power to reframe the way you and your team approach customers.

An NSP is not a tactic. It's a *strategic shift* in the way you approach your business. It's more than a simple sales technique; it's a sales leadership approach that turbocharges all other techniques. It's the missing ingredient a sales force needs to take their performance to the next level.

You gain the following from approaching sales with an NSP mindset:

- You become more resourceful as a salesperson, since you're always looking for ways to help customers' businesses.
- Clients take you to the higher-level people in their organizations, because they see you as a resource and not someone with a sales quota.
- You establish relationships with these higher-level people, because you will have greater impact there.
- You have a shorter sales cycle. You ask more robust and second-tier questions, delving into critical customer business issues, whereas product-focused people ask low-level manipulative and mechanical questions.
- You create proposals and presentations that are more persuasive, because they're organized around the client's goals, not focused on *your* product's or service's features and benefits.
- You increase the probability of success with the current opportunity, as well as future opportunities, because you understand the client's organizational direction.
- You're less likely to be seen as a commodity and have pricing issues, because you can map everything to the client's urgent business goals.

- You love your job, because you have a more noble purpose than just "selling stuff to make money."

- Your job becomes far more interesting, because every opportunity requires new thinking and solutions and is a chance to make a difference.

- You're more likely to talk about your job in social situations, and when you do, people are more likely to be interested in hearing about it—since making a difference in people's lives is exciting.

- You bring the customer's voice into your organization, which helps you create better products, services, and marketing.

- You get better coaching from your boss, because your conversations are about topics deeper than quotas. You speak in depth about client situations and needs.

- You gain a competitive advantage, because your work becomes a noble calling.

- You don't have to "act like" you care about your customers, because you really *do* care.

- You're better able to manage obstacles, because you don't get defensive and take them personally. You see them for what they are: a simple request for help.

- You know what really matters to customers; you don't trot out trite or artificial differentiators.

- Your work has a larger purpose. Your NSP becomes your North Star, a way of resetting yourself during tough times.

How to Use This Book

I want to make this extremely clear: This is not a book about marketing. This is a book about **sales**. An NSP is not a tagline. It's a tool that sales leaders can use at every level of their operation to grow revenue and do work that makes everyone in the organization proud.

The ideas and techniques you'll learn in this book are drawn from the more than 10,000 hours I and my colleagues have spent studying, coaching, training, observing, and interviewing salespeople and sales managers. In addition to observing their behavior, I've also conducted in-depth interviews to uncover their mindsets, attitudes, and beliefs.

I've been in this business for more than 25 years and have worked with some of the best sales organizations in the world. I've coached and trained sales leaders from Apple, Google, Kimberly-Clark, Pfizer, Procter & Gamble, and a host of other top companies. Whether you work for a global giant or a small firm that's just getting started, you can apply the ideas in this book to your sales efforts right away.

This book is meant to be practical, not just theory. I want you to be a better sales leader *tomorrow*. As such, at the end of each chapter, I've included a feature I call "Do One Thing"—a single idea that you can implement immediately.

The book is divided into three parts. In the first part you'll learn how NSP works and why it makes such a difference in sales performance. I'll explain the three elements of an effective NSP and provide you with examples from my clients and others. You'll see how leaders in a range of careers and industries—banking, construction, health care, IT, manufacturing, and even a California court system— have used this process to jump-start their organizations. We'll look at some surprising information about why overemphasizing profit has an alarming effect on salespeople and customers and how you can reframe the profit question inside your company. You'll learn some of the brain science behind NSP and where it fits within the structure of your larger organization. At the conclusion of this section, we'll walk through a three-part process to help you create your own NSP.

The second part of the book is where the rubber meets the road—because as we all know, ideas don't work unless you put them into practice. This is where you'll learn how to keep your NSP alive in the face of daily challenges. We'll look at the role that fear plays in selling and how it erodes your NSP. You'll learn techniques to keep that from happening to your team. You'll discover some surprising science about the impact that mindset has on salespeople and customers, and you'll learn five NSP mindsets that will make you and your team more powerful. We'll also look at why most of the time and money we spend on sales training is wasted and how you can avoid that costly pitfall in the future.

We'll explore the role of customer information in the sales process. You'll discover why some of the very systems meant to improve sales performance, such as your CRM, may be undermining sales performance in ways that you don't realize. You'll learn techniques for creating compelling NSP stories and case studies to substantiate your NSP with customers and your team.

You'll learn coaching techniques that will dramatically improve your sales reps' performance on sales calls. We'll look at how you can use your NSP with your marketing team and internally to invigorate projects and alleviate turf wars and silos. You'll also learn how one pivotal behavior can put your entire organization on the path toward an NSP.

The third part of the book is the road warrior's bible: a sales manager's blueprint for creating a sales force of true believers. Each of the short chapters in this section focuses on a single area of sales manager responsibility: sales meetings, incentive programs, interviews, presentations, and precall coaching, among others. You'll learn how to apply specific techniques for using your NSP in each of these areas, how to bring your NSP to life in sales meetings, and how to use it during interviews to quickly identify top performers (and nonperformers). You'll learn how to reinforce your NSP with visual reminders and how to coach salespeople right before they begin an important call.

At the end of this book, I've included a bonus chapter, "How to Use Purpose to Make the Rest of Your Life More Meaningful." I'll also share the personal story about the painful experience that taught me some of these lessons the hard way.

Here's what you can expect from me:

- **I'll give you the best of what I've got**. You hold in your hands the result of 25 years spent studying, coaching, training, and interviewing salespeople, sales managers, and their customers. I've combined my experience with the latest research about human behavior to give you practical tools and techniques that you can use starting tomorrow.

- **I'll provide real-life examples**. It's challenging to go from concept to application, so this book is filled with examples from major corporations such as Procter & Gamble and Southwest Airlines, along with smaller firms such as getAbstract and Graham-White—two sales forces that are now using NSP to become market leaders. You'll see how sales leaders just like you have adopted this process to jump-start their teams.

- **I'll share stories about failure**. Instances where I and others have missed the mark—in some cases, horribly so—will show you what *not* to do. You'll also discover that no matter how bad things seem at the time, it's never too late to reclaim your noble purpose.
- **I'll ask provoking questions**. I want you to think deeply about what your job means to the world. So I'll ask you to consider your work in ways that might be unfamiliar to you. I want you to be great at your job. I also want you to enjoy it.
- **I'll honor your intelligence**. You wouldn't be holding this book if you hadn't already achieved some level of success, since this book wasn't written for the sales novice. It's for people who are serious about sales leadership and who want to take their teams and themselves to the next level.

Reframing the Sales Profession

I have high aspirations for you and for our profession. For me, this is personal. As the famous saying goes, nothing happens until somebody sells something. Salespeople are linchpins; we're the ones who bring in the revenue that keeps everything else running. Personally, I believe that a role in sales is one of the highest callings you can have in an organization.

Unfortunately, our profession doesn't always get the respect it deserves. There are two widespread misperceptions about sales:

1. Sales is sleazy.
2. Sales is easy.

Scott Jensen, a sales coach at Deloitte, tells a story about being a young sales manager with another company. Upon walking into an internal departmental company meeting, he heard one of the other department heads say, "Here comes the commission whore." The rest of the group laughed at the joke.

I am not kidding when I say that this story makes my head spin. I feel tightness in my chest when someone insults a fellow salesperson; my heart starts to beat faster, and I feel an anger akin to what you'd feel if someone offended a member of your family.

I completely understand why salespeople sometimes get a bad rap. The bad ones can be pushy, arrogant, and downright awful. But that doesn't describe the salespeople I know.

The salespeople I know return customer calls at 7 o'clock on Friday night because they care about their clients. They leave before sunrise so that they can be in a customer's office for an early meeting. They stand for hours at trade shows, enthusiastically engaging every person who comes up to the booth. They make sales calls at all hours of the day. They go in at 5 AM to meet the end users. They visit customer sites on the weekend. They work a full day in the field and head home to do their paperwork at night. They work on presentations at 10 PM, after they put their kids to bed.

They put thousands of miles on their boxy four-door cars. They squeeze themselves into the center seat of a packed plane for a 4-hour commute to the next city after a long day in the field. They spend evenings away from their families hunched over computers in lonely hotel rooms. They study sales reports for hours, trying to figure out how they can reach even more customers next year. They do most of their work alone and often have to motivate themselves in the face of rejection. They even smile when customers are rude to them.

And they do all of this to make a living for their families and create success for their organizations. If you're one of those kinds of sales professionals, this book is for you. If want to build a team of top performers that you can be proud of, people who make a difference to their customers and who drive revenue through the roof, you're in the right place.

If you want to manipulate customers or lead by fear and intimidation—well, then, you're not.

I love salespeople. They're the unsung heroes of business, and I want to restore nobility to the sales profession.

This is a book to help you think and act. Therefore, this is what I ask of you:

- **Give this your best effort**. This approach requires a shift in thinking that may not seem natural at first. But it works. What may seem artificial initially will become second nature with a little practice.
- **Read Part I in order**. After that, you can jump around. The subsequent chapters are written as stand-alone sections, so pick whatever interests you and start there.

- **Write things down**. There are several places where you'll be asked critical questions. We've provided space for your answers. Write them down. (E-book readers can use a scratch pad.) Writing things down will help you remember what you've said and will increase the clarity of your thoughts.

- **Do *something*.** The book is filled with easy-to-implement action items. Pick the one that seems the easiest for you and do it first. If you experience some success right off the bat, you'll be more likely to stick with it.

- **Don't give up**. As a sales leader, you have the power to change the culture around you. It may sometimes seem as though your customers, team, industry, and perhaps even your boss are working against you. But I promise you this: you will begin to see a shift in the people around if you use these techniques. It almost always happens faster than you expect.

Whether you're leading a large organization or running a small group, this book will help you find your NSP and ignite it with your customers and team. You'll learn how to drive more sales revenue and enjoy your job more while you're doing it.

I'm going to let you in on a secret: your life is about much more than just making money. It's about the impact you have on other people. As a sales leader, you have the opportunity to interact with more people in a month than most people do in a year. Every word you say and every action you take has a ripple effect on the people around you.

Don't ever think for a moment that your job doesn't matter. It *does*.

You already make a difference, and I want to help you make an even bigger difference. When you know that your job matters, you perform at a higher level and enjoy it more. I told you that I wanted to help you like your job, but that's not entirely true. I don't want you to merely *like* your job; I want you to love your job. When you love your job, your whole life lights up—and so does everyone around you.

You deserve that. We all do.

Are you ready to get started?

CHAPTER

2

Why Noble Sales Purpose Works

Great minds have purpose, others have wishes.

—Washington Irving

Imagine you're at a neighborhood party or standing on the sidelines of a kid's soccer game. You engage in a conversation with the person next to you, and he asks the age-old question, "What do you do for a living?"

How do you answer? You've likely been asked the question a hundred times, so you probably have a standard answer. If you're alone right now, say it out loud. If you're reading this book on a plane or in a coffee shop, just mumble your answer under your breath.

Then pay attention to how you feel saying those words.

If you're like most people, you probably give a fairly rote response that doesn't require much thinking: something along the lines of, "I sell software" or "I'm regional manager for XYZ Company." If you work for an impressive firm or you have an impressive title, you may have said, "I run a sales team for Google" or "I'm the VP of sales at Clorox." But it's usually still a pretty standard answer.

Again, remember how it felt to say those words out loud. This is your baseline.

Now we're going to go a bit deeper.

I'd like you to think about a time when you made a difference at work. Perhaps you helped someone on your team, did something great for a customer, or lent an ear when a colleague needed to vent. It may have happened in your current job, or it may have been in a past job. Either one is fine.

Recall this situation and write down some notes to help you remember it more clearly. You won't experience the shift if you just read through this quickly, so I encourage you to record the answers to these questions:

- What was the situation?
- How did you make a difference?
- What did the other person say?
- How did he or she look?
- How did you feel afterward?

Now imagine yourself telling this story out loud. In fact, if you have a friend or colleague nearby, tell that person the story. If not, say it out loud to yourself—or at least pretend you are.

Now, compare how you felt in the first scenario, when you described what you did for a living, with how you felt in the second scenario, where you told a story about making a difference.

What do you notice?

How was the second time different from the first time? Which one did you *enjoy* talking about more? Which one was more engaging? Which one made you prouder? And which one would you rather *listen to* if you were on the other end?

Pay careful attention to the difference between the two and how you felt in each scenario, because most people experience a pretty dramatic difference.

I do this activity in my programs by asking people first to tell the person next to them what they do for a living and then to describe a time they made a difference at work. The difference between the two experiences is startling. When I ask groups to compare them, I hear things like:

> "The first time was a no-brainer, but the second time I was totally into it."
>
> "The first time was boring; the second time was more emotional."
>
> "I was on autopilot the first time, but the second time it was like I was reliving the experience again."

One vice president (VP) of sales even said, "The first time I thought it; the second time I felt it. The first time was flat; the second time I was passionate."

That's a pretty accurate description of what happens to your brain.

The first time—when you describe your job—you're using your brain at a very basic level, almost on autopilot. The second time, when you describe making a difference, you likely ignited your frontal lobe. This is the part of the brain associated with reasoning, planning, problem solving, language, and higher-level emotions such as empathy and altruism.

Describing the meaningful impact you had on another person engages a higher-level part of your brain than when you describe your job. As such, this is what I observe when people do this exercise: When people talk about what they do for a living, they

- Smile politely.
- Use rote language, such as *reseller, provider, end-to-end solutions, implement,* and so on.
- Sit relatively still.

And the listeners nod nicely.

However, when people describe making a difference, they

- Smile with their whole faces.
- Use colorful details, such as describing the look on someone's face or the setting.
- Become much more animated and describe the impact they had on someone.

And their listeners lean in and ask questions.

I ask the two questions within 5 minutes of each other. When you stand on the stage watching people respond, you'd think it was an entirely different day. Sometimes they even look like an entirely different group of people.

The first time it's just a regular crowd of businesspeople politely speaking to one another in low voices. The second time, volume cranks up. The people get engaged. They start laughing. Some people even stand up when they tell the second story. They can't help themselves.

The first time, people are just going through the motions. The second time, they're animated and alive. There's more energy and enthusiasm in the air. When you watch them the second time, you'd think they'd just won lottery or heard some great news. And in a way, *they did.* By describing how they made a difference to someone, they got the best payoff a human being can have: they were reminded of just how much their life matters.

The Two Big Human Needs: Connection and Meaning

Beyond basic needs such as food and shelter, human beings have two core emotional needs: connection and meaning. We want to be connected to other people, and we want to know that what we're doing matters to someone. The need for belonging and significance transcends age, culture, sex, race, and socioeconomic status.

Our deepest desire is to make a difference in the world—and our darkest fear is that we won't.

We don't just want to make a difference in our personal lives or through philanthropic activities. We want to make a difference at work. After all, this is what we do all day, every day. People are desperate to be part of something bigger than themselves. When you know that your job matters to people, you come alive. Your frontal lobes light up, and you have greater access to problem solving, language, and empathy.

The exercise you just did—one that I've done with thousands of people around the world—proves that we *can* ignite that passion at work.

Yet for some reason, we all seem to operate according to this bizarre notion that emotions don't belong in the workplace. This is total bunk. When was the last time you heard a CEO say, "I wish my people weren't so motivated and excited?"

How can you possibly get people engaged and excited without connecting to them emotionally? Igniting positive emotions with your team and customers gives you a huge competitive advantage.

You read in the introduction about a top-performing biotech salesperson who outsold every other rep in the entire country three years running. She achieved this because every day when she went on calls, she remembered a grandmother she had helped.

Thinking about the grandmother did more than just motivate this sales rep to make extra sales call on a rainy Friday afternoon. It ignited her frontal lobe, which made her a better problem solver and strategic planner, more skilled with language, and more empathetic with her customers.

Is it any wonder that she was the number one rep three years running? Her peers and competitors were likely conducting sales calls with the basic parts of their brain, going through the motions mechanically without igniting any passion. But because she was thinking about the person she had helped—the grandmother who, because of her product, could now play with her grandkids and travel when she wanted—the top rep was leveraging her intellect and her emotions to their fullest extent.

A Noble Sales Purpose (NSP) is the secret of igniting that type of higher-level thinking with everyone on your team. It serves as an organizing element for your sales force. It keeps you focused on the big picture.

It's your version of the grandmother.

Most salespeople don't carry into their sales calls a clear picture of the ultimate impact they have on customers. That's why your job as a leader is to proactively help them generate that mental picture.

An NSP answers three questions:

1. What impact do you and your company have on customers?
2. How are you different from the competition?
3. On your best day, what do you love about your job?

An NSP is not "We're going to be the number one provider of end-to-end solutions." That's *your* goal, and it doesn't speak to how you make a difference in *clients'* lives. An NSP isn't about your desired position in the market. It's about how you impact your clients today.

That's the litmus test: How do we make a difference to our customers?

10 Sample NSPs

The following pages provide several examples of real companies that drive great results by using an NSP. Keep in mind as you read these examples that crafting your NSP is only the start of the process. You'll eventually use it to improve customer interactions, sales forecasting, coaching, and presentations—and likely even your comp plan and customer relationship management (CRM). Crafting your NSP is the reframe that begins the process.

Think of it this way. Imagine you're sitting in a jet parked on a runway at Chicago's O'Hare airport and it's pointed toward Tucson. If you alter the direction of that jet by 10 degrees to the west, you wind up at a totally different destination: instead of Tucson, you end up in Hawaii. This is how just a small shift at the start of the journey puts you on an entirely new trajectory.

Establishing your NSP is this small shift. Your NSP is the reframe that prompts you to start looking in completely different places for solutions and that will take you to a new destination.

The companies described in this chapter are achieving great results because of what their NSP says and how they're using it.

Meridian Systems: A Shift from Product Centric to Customer

Meridian is a Folsom, California–based company that sells project management software for the building industry. Their software helps buildings go up faster, safer, and more economically. Their *goal* is to "Become the number one provider of project management software in the world."

The construction industry is tough. Meridian's general manager Geene Alhady was challenged to get everyone on board with the shift. He says, "When we sell the deal, it's a celebration, but then afterward it becomes just work. We want to communicate to our team your work is meaningful; it's not just a bunch of problems."

Alhady says, "We went through a time when our customers were saying, you have great visions, but then the execution was not there. When we were smaller, the sales guys were directly connected with the development. We all bled this passion for changing the way the industry builds things. Then the original team left, and we gradually we lost our identification with the passion for the industry. We needed to change that."

Alhady needed to help Meridian reclaim their passion. Working with their senior leaders we came up with the following NSP as a result:

We help people build a better world.

Their NSP behaviors are:

We connect.
We collaborate.
We care.

The first goal is about their desired market position. Their NSP speaks to the impact they have on customers.

And they don't just say it. They're *passionate* about it. They drive by buildings, pointing them out to their kids, saying, "Look—we're part of that." Their sales force is on fire, because they're improving the way buildings, as they put it, "come out of the ground."

Alhady repeats their NSP at the start of every single meeting to remind the team why they're in business. Meridian's NSP is propelling them very quickly back to market leadership.

Graham-White Manufacturing: A Shift from Product to Customer

Graham-White is the world's technology leader in the drying of compressed air for locomotives and rail transit vehicles. Admittedly, this might not sound like the sexiest business, but it's necessary. If you're on a train and moisture gets into the air system, cold temperatures will cause the moisture to freeze, the brakes won't function properly, and the train won't move.

Graham-White is a 98-year-old Virginia-based company with a long, rich history of providing components to the transportation systems that millions of people depend on every day. Their salespeople call on engineers and purchasing groups at customers such as Amtrak, GE Transportation, Union Pacific, and New York City Transit.

Graham-White's tagline used to be, "We provide reliable transportation solutions."

It's a good tagline, but it didn't speak to the impact they have on customers. So we worked with their sales leadership team to reframe their tagline into a true NSP:

We help make transportation safer, faster, and more reliable.

The difference is subtle; it's also significant. The first tagline described their products. Their new NSP describes the impact that their products have on the customers.

Now instead of starting their sales calls with a description of their solutions, they begin by asking the customer questions about their environment, goals, and challenges. This allows them to understand exactly what safety, efficiency, and reliability mean to that particular customer.

VP of sales Stewart Bruce says, "Moving to an NSP shifted us from a product focus to a customer focus. It moved the conversation from cost to value; even tough buyers like purchasing departments respond differently."

Graham-White uses stories about how they kept a locomotive brake system from freezing up or kept trains running during a hard freeze to substantiate their NSP. These compelling concrete examples show precisely how they really *do* make transportation safer, faster, and more reliable.

The company's NSP approach has helped them win several million-dollar contracts, because they hone in on making it come alive for each individual customer.

CMIT Solutions: From IT Provider to Business Partner

CMIT Solutions is a franchise organization that provides managed information technology (IT) services for small businesses. With 140 locations in North America, they have a great brand. Yet the individual franchisees in each market determine how they approach their customers.

Many of their franchisees come from a technical background and don't have much sales experience. When asked to describe themselves, they typically say, "We provide IT solutions for small businesses."

Yet our interviews with their most successful franchisees revealed that CMIT does much more than just provide IT services. They alleviate one of the biggest headaches in business: system problems. We worked with their corporate team to craft a simple statement that reflects their aspirations for their customers:

We help make small businesses more successful.

CEO Jeff Connally says, "We went from 'We sell IT services' to 'We help make small businesses more successful.' That seemingly simple reframe changed everything for us. Our guys feel like the White Knights of the IT world. They're going after new business with a zeal they never had before. Our year over year sales are up by 35 percent."

Changing their focus from the services they provide to the impact they have on clients created a shift in the way CMIT approaches customers. According to Connally, "Our people are technical, so their tendency is to jump right into the tech stuff. Now, instead of [taking that approach], we take a step back and address the situation from a business perspective."

Connally explains, "We pulled our NSP to the front and center of everything we do. It helped move our franchisees from simply being IT providers into a partnership role. [They now realize that] their purpose isn't just to sell IT services; it's to help their customers be more successful."

In a challenging economy when many organizations are cutting back on outside IT support, CMIT continues to grow revenue.

getAbstract: Less Is More

getAbstract, Inc., is the world's largest library of business book summaries. They provide five-page abstracts of popular business books to fast track learning and development. The company literature describes it this way: "getAbstract's mission is to find, expertly compress and provide universal access to critical business knowledge, in a format that can be quickly and easily absorbed, allowing our customers to stay current, competitive and to become leaders who can make better decisions. Today, our solutions include a library of more than 8,000 business book summaries, used by over 10 million subscribers, including 20 percent of the Fortune 500."

getAbstract, CEO Michel Koopman and the getAbstract sales force are passionate about the power of knowledge. Their compressed knowledge helps their subscribers stay current and competitive and become leaders who can make better decisions. We created their NSP during their 2012 national sales meeting. Their 25 salespeople and I spent an afternoon honing in on their highest aspirations for their clients, and they came up with the following:

We turn employees into leaders.

Sometimes less is more. The statement in their literature is a description of who getAbstract is, what they do, and who their customers are. It describes their client base and business model.

getAbstract's statement after finding their NSP is simple and elegant and describes the impact they have on clients. It's the starting point that propels their sales force to go beyond the obvious surface benefits and dig deeply into customer business issues.

Koopman says, "Even if you walk into the meeting thinking, 'I'm here to turn employees into leaders,' you're still selling yourself short—because you're only going to listen to answers that you are looking for. You're waiting to hear the answers that are aligned with that purpose. When you meet with a top leader, you should actually take a step back and have a conversation to find out what makes that person successful at that level."

Koopman is known among his sales team for asking, "What are we doing for our customers? What internal initiatives are we helping them with? How are we improving their results?" He says, "[We're a smaller organization, so we] don't have a CMO [chief marketing officer] or a strategist to reinforce the purpose. As the CEO, I have to reinforce the purpose and the revenue goals."

As of this writing, getAbstract's sales are up 80 percent year to date, and they're ahead of plan by 18 percent.

Orange County Court: Simple Elegance

Many companies tend to try to "kitchen sink" their NSP—that is, to throw in every single thing you could possibly do for customers. But it's important to fight the temptation to overdescribe, because a simple statement is much more powerful.

One of my favorite examples of simple elegance comes from California's Orange County Court system. Their NSP is:

We Unclog the Wheels of Justice.

You might not think of a court system as having customers, but the Orange County Court believes they do. They consider the plaintiffs, the defendants, the jurors, and the lawyers all their customers. Their NSP speaks to their desire to make a difference in people's lives during times of conflict and stress. They strive to implement the principles of our country in a just, fair, and efficient way for all parties involved.

Interestingly, Orange County's NSP didn't come down from the executive team. It came from a single person. During a leadership program, I asked the group of 60 people divided among eight tables to discuss how they make a difference to customers. When the teams were sharing results, one of their in-house attorneys stared at the lists on the flip charts and said, "You know what we do? We unclog the wheels of justice."

You could have heard a pin drop in that room after she said it. Sixty people sat taller in their chairs, smiling because they knew their jobs mattered. I swear that I even saw some of them start to get misty-eyed.

These words spoke to the highest aspirations of everyone in the room. That single powerful statement contained what Jim Collins refers to in *Good to Great* as "the quiet ping of truth like a single, clear, perfectly struck note hanging in the air in the hushed silence of a full auditorium at the end of a quiet movement of a Mozart piano concerto."

An ideal NSP is not full of bravado or bluster; it's not something you *hope* to do. It's something you *can* do, right now. It's fully within your grasp, and every person in the room knows it. It doesn't require explaining or defending, because it taps into what you're already doing and what you want to do more of.

I find Orange County Court's NSP positively breathtaking. When you combine NSP thinking with the principles from our founding fathers, I too get misty-eyed.

But Orange County Court's NSP does more than just make a patriotic heart beat faster; there are practical applications. Their NSP—"We Unclog the Wheels of Justice"—is also helping them deal with extreme budget cuts. When most organizations face a budget crisis, the question becomes, "How can we cut?" But Orange Country's NSP prompts them to ask, "How can we continue to unclog the wheels of justice with a lot less budget?"

That reframe keeps them focused on the end game. It prevents the turf battles that usually occur during budget cuts because everyone agrees on the NSP.

You Don't Have to Create World Peace

You'll notice that none of the preceding examples include developing lifesaving drugs or creating world peace. They come from five very different organizations in industries whose products (software, air compressors, IT support, book abstracts, and court services) don't necessarily scream "excitement." I intentionally chose these organizations to demonstrate how seemingly ordinary companies have used this process. Someone outside these industries might think that these organizations are just ordinary business-to-business (B2B) sellers or bureaucracies that don't make a big difference to their customers. But when you dig a little deeper, you discover that they *do* make a difference. And the same is true for you and your organization.

These examples demonstrate that no matter what you sell, you can always find your NSP. The NSP concept can be applied to almost any industry or product.

Why Mission and Vision
Aren't Enough

Mission and vision statements can be compelling. But more often than not, they're internally focused. In his book, *Grow: How Ideals Power Growth and Profit at the World's Great Companies*, former Procter & Gamble (P&G) CMO Jim Stengel writes, "When you strip away the platitudes from those documents, what's left typically boils down to: 'We want our current business model to make or keep us the leader of our current pack of competitors in current and immediately foreseeable market conditions.'"

The traditional mission and vision is a formula for mediocrity, says Stengel. "It aims too low, locking an enterprise into a business model based on the agenda of the business, not that of the customer. If such a statement mentions the customer at all, it's the customer as seen from the company's point of view and in terms of the company's agenda."

I was a sales manager for P&G during the late 1980s, when Stengel was a rising star in marketing. During my tenure at P&G, I saw our stock rise and split, delivering a 199 percent return between 1985 and 1990. But by 2000, P&G was in trouble. The company lost $85 billion in market capitalization in only six months. Stengel says, "P&G's core businesses were stagnating and its people were demoralized."

Great brands weren't enough. P&G's people needed a purpose. A.G. Lafley, then the CEO, asked Stengel to take on the role of global marketing officer to help transform the culture of the company to one wherein "the consumer is boss."

Stengel says, "To hit these big targets, we needed an even bigger goal: identifying and activating a distinctive ideal (or *purpose*, as P&G dubbed it). Improving people's lives would be the explicit goal of every business in the P&G portfolio. We could then establish each business's true reason for being as the basis for new growth, and we could link them all into a strong foundation for P&G's recovery by building each business's culture around its ideal."

Stengel writes, "A.G. Lafley and I—along with the rest of the senior management team—expected each business leader to articulate how each brand's individual identity furthered P&G's overarching mantra of improving people's lives. We also had to model the ideal ourselves. And we had to measure all our activities and people in terms of the ideals of our brands and the company as a whole. The success of that effort brought P&G's extraordinary growth from 2001 on."

Identifying a larger purpose put P&G back on course. The 175-year-old consumer giant remains one of the most admired companies in the world. The company's story demonstrates that no matter how big you are, or how long you've been in business, you can always reclaim your noble purpose.

Southwest Airlines is another example of a well-known industry leader founded on a noble purpose.

Founder Herb Kelleher has made Southwest's purpose absolutely clear: to democratize the skies. Marketing expert Roy Spence, who works with Kelleher, says that Southwest is in the freedom business. They have a mission and vision, but their purpose, "democratize the skies," trumps everything.

Spence explains it this way in his book, *It's Not What You Sell, It's What You Stand For:*

> *Purpose* is the difference you're trying to make.
> *Mission* is how you do it.
> *Vision* is how you see the world after you've done your
>   purpose and mission.

He then illustrates how it works at Southwest:

Purpose: "Southwest Airlines is democratizing the skies."
Mission: "We democratize the skies by keeping our fares low and spirits high."
Vision: "I see a world in which everyone in America has the chance to go and see and do things they've never dreamed of—where everyone has the ability to fly."

During a challenging economic time, when their competitors are grasping for straws, Southwest's clarity of purpose acts as a filter to help them make better decisions. It's their North Star. They spend money only on the things that matter: safety, airplanes, people, and locations. Southwest's purpose—"democratize the skies"—is infused at every level of the organization, including sales and customer service.

In a recent keynote that was broadcasted on YouTube, Spence tells a story from several years ago. Consultants came into Southwest and said if they start charging for bags, they would immediately drop $350 million to the bottom line. "All the others are doing it," the consultants said, and Southwest could make a fast profit if they did the same.

Senior leaders Dave Ridley, Gary Kelly, and others said, "No, that violates the purpose of our company," and instructed the team to "go find the money." Charging for bags wouldn't give more people the chance to fly; in fact, it would make the skies *less* accessible.

Spence describes the situation, "But you'll make more money," said the consultants and finance team. The answer was still, "No. It doesn't serve our purpose." Ultimately, Southwest's refusal to stray from their purpose made them money instead of costing them. They launched an ad campaign called "Bags fly free." Nine months later, the senior leadership team met and the financial people said, "We made a mistake." By running the ad campaign and sticking to their purpose, Southwest drove $1 billion in new revenue, taking additional share from their competitors.

You can watch Roy Spence tell the Southwest's purpose story on YouTube. My favorite part starts at minute 37; the smirk on Spence's face as he describes how purpose made Southwest more profitable is priceless.

An NSP keeps you focused on what matters: the customer.

The Google Sales Reframe

Sometimes even the most powerful mission statements require a reframe for the sales force. Consider Google, whose well-known mission statement is "to organize the world's information and make it universally accessible and useful."

Google's mission isn't empty words on a plaque about market leadership. It's about how they make a difference in the world, and their employees live and breathe it. Many people have heard the tales about what an amazing place Google is to work. Some of their well-known perks include on-site chefs, free lunch, and pool tables in the conference room. Their Zurich office and others even have slides that take you from one floor to the next. But behind the exterior cool factor is a global team of people who are on fire for their jobs.

Google's mission is real and powerful. Yet it still needs to be translated for sales—particularly for the B2B salespeople who sell advertising to major corporations such as Home Depot and Nordstrom.

During a recent Selling with Noble Purpose program I conducted at their Atlanta sales office, one of the top sales performers told me, "I'm passionate about our mission statement, but it's easy to think of myself as just the money person—the one who delivers the sales so everyone else can achieve the mission."

Translating Google's mission into an NSP meant focusing on the individual business customer. This particular group of salespeople recognized that their NSP is to help "organize *our clients'* information and make it universally accessible and useful." The slight tweak is important, because the salespeople need to be focused on the individual client's information—not the world's—during sales calls.

Even if you have a powerful mission statement, you still need an NSP. A visionary picture of the future isn't enough. Salespeople need to know, "How can I make a difference to this customer *today?*" Your NSP ensures that everything you do—and every decision you make—is aligned with the impact you want to have on customers.

If you don't have a mission and vision statement, or if—be honest—they're meaningless platitudes filled with jargon, then don't worry. An NSP is enough. This is because an NSP gives salespeople a reason to get out of bed right now. It keeps them focused on the opportunities that are in front of them today. It elevates sales performance with customers immediately.

Now NSP Drives Shareholder Value

I was working with a CEO of an international family-owned bank in Bermuda, Capital G. The President and CEO, Ian Truran, is a great guy who has worked his way up through the organization to the CEO position. He's well-liked by his team and is a very public figure in the community.

When we initially discussed Capital G's purpose, Truran said, "Our primary purpose is to deliver value to our shareholders."

It's a common assertion for CEO's because that's what their board expects. Delivering shareholder value is job number one for a CEO. But delivering shareholder value isn't concrete or meaningful enough to direct the daily actions of line employees.

In discussing Cap G's purpose, I asked Ian, "Would delivering shareholder be meaningful to a business banking representative, or a teller?"

He laughed and said, "Of course not."

He's a smart man. The employees of the bank truly love and admire the family members who own the bank, and they want to deliver results for them. But even so, "delivering shareholder value" isn't something employees can wrap their arms around every day at work.

Working with Truran and his senior team, Cap G now has the following NSP:

We help people achieve financial success.

"People" includes customers, the employees, and the family shareholders. It's important that owners achieve financial success so that the bank can keep running. By helping their clients achieve financial success, they ensure that the shareholders and employees achieve financial success as well.

Their NSP values follow:

We deliver value.

We build trust.

We act with integrity.

We are a family.

It's no coincidence that Capital G was ranked number one in their market for customer service, beating out a major bigger name bank. Their NSP, along with their values, keeps them focused on their customers.

Shareholders versus Stakeholders

Shareholders are not stakeholders. Shareholders don't make sales calls; they're not required to go the extra mile, and they don't interact with customers. Shareholders invest because they expect a return on their money. Passion is not a requirement for shareholders.

Passion, however, is a must for stakeholders. The stakeholders are the employees responsible for delivering shareholder value.

A strong NSP doesn't distract you from delivering shareholder value. In fact, it enables you to do an even better job of it.

The Business Case for NSP

Purpose and value driven organizations outperform the market by 15:1—and outperform comparison companies by 6:1.

—Jim Collins & Jerry Porrass
(*Built to Last* and *Good to Great*)

Organizations who center their business on improving people's lives have a growth rate triple that of their competitors.

—Millward Brown Optimor 10-year
growth study of over 50,000 brands done
in partnership with Jim Stengel (*Grow*)

Salespeople who sell with noble purpose—who want to make a difference to customers—outsell salespeople who focus on sales goals and money.

—McLeod & More, Inc. six-year study
of top-performing salespeople

The Motley Fool is a well-known financial services company whose purpose is "To Help the World Invest. Better." Their analysts recommend that investors who want a strong return on their investment look for companies with a strong sense of purpose. As Motley Fool equity analyst Todd Wenning writes in a 2012 article on their site, "The greatest stock of the next generation will be companies with a tremendous sense of purpose led by passionate executives who are guided by that purpose—and not solely by profits."

Citing such past great stock picks like Google and Whole Foods, Wenning writes, "I like maximizing shareholder value as much as the next investor, but I'm concerned with maximizing *long-term* shareholder value, and that requires a business purpose that can carry on for decades, not quarters."

A study by Harvard Business School faculty member John Kotter and James Heskett found that purpose-driven companies experience many benefits:

1. Lower employee turnover, which keeps costs low
2. Higher productivity, which leads to superior efficiency
3. Better pricing power, which helps maintain profits

Beyond the obvious financial benefits, having a purpose gives more meaning to your job, which, in turn, gives more meaning to your life. When you have a purpose that matters, you become more effective and productive on every level.

Yes, an NSP makes you money. It also makes you happy.

Do One Thing

Do the exercise at the beginning of this chapter and ask yourself, "When did I make a difference to a customer?" Ask your team the same question. Sharing these stories is how you start reframing the narrative of your organization.

CHAPTER
3

Why *Profit* Is Not a Purpose

To have no set purpose in one's life is harlotry of the will.
—Stephen MacKenna

In February 2012, former Goldman Sachs executive director Greg Smith announced, via a scathing op-ed for the *New York Times*, that he was resigning after 12 years at Goldman because "the interests of the client continue to be sidelined in the way the firm operates and thinks about making money."

Smith wrote, "Not one single minute is spent asking questions about how we can help clients. It's purely about how we can make the most possible money off of them. If you were an alien from Mars and sat in on one of these meetings, you would believe that a client's success or progress was not part of the thought process at all."

Ouch.

Smith's op-ed about Goldman Sachs was the *Times* most e-mailed article for several days in a row. Goldman saw $2.15 billion of its market value wiped out as a result of the letter.

Double ouch.

Smith's op-ed went viral because it confirmed what people had long suspected about Goldman and other brokers: they didn't care about the clients; they cared only about the money.

How Overemphasizing Profit Erodes Your Bottom Line

When leaders believe that their sole purpose is to produce profit, they view their customers as "its." Customers are no longer human beings; they are anonymous targets and prospects whose sole purpose is to help the company make money.

Smith described a culture very much like this at Goldman, where leaders routinely referred to customers in disparaging manipulative terms. He wrote, "Over the last 12 months, I have seen five different managing directors refer to their own clients as 'Muppets,' sometimes over internal e-mail."

The way leaders talk about customers *matters*. When you emphasize short-term profit over long-term customer satisfaction, employees get the message loud and clear. A junior employee who hears his boss call customers Muppets isn't going to take those customers' needs and concerns very seriously in the future. And this is fatal for a sales force.

The internal conversation always becomes the external conversation. It doesn't always wind up in the *New York Times*, but it does show up in how your people treat your customers.

A Noble Sales Purpose (NSP) keeps your customers from becoming "its." A company with a strong NSP would never allow anyone, *especially not a senior leader*, to refer to their customers as Muppets. I suspect there are more than a few Goldman customers reflecting back on their conversations with their account manager wondering, "Does he think I'm a dumb Muppet?"

Most decent leaders don't make a practice of using disparaging names for customers, but talking about customers as anonymous targets and prospects isn't much better. When leaders talk about customers solely as a means to achieve their own goals, it radiates out to every single person in the organization. That kind of language creates a culture that says, "We don't exist to do something for our customers; customers exist to do something for *us*."

People no longer care about helping customers; they just want to make money off of them. And it's only a matter of time before the customers start to feel it.

Imagine what would happen if Goldman had an NSP. What if instead of focusing solely on profit, the company's higher purpose was to serve customers?

How might the internal conversations go? How would that affect their product development and their marketing? How would they evaluate their leaders? Would they alter their hiring profiles? What criteria would be the most important?

What would happen if the leaders talked about customers as people they want to help rather than targets they want to close? How would that affect the sales force and the customer service people?

What impact would it have on customers? What would happen to their stock price?

I'll tell you exactly what would happen. When you decide that your higher purpose is serving customers, you create a company like Apple, Disney, Merck, Procter & Gamble, or Southwest Airlines. These are organizations that generate sustained profits because they hold their customers in high regard. They drive revenue *and* do work that makes them proud.

Temple University ethics professor Steven Nevin Pyser says, "If you look at Enron or WorldCom or Tyco or Goldman Sachs, you can have well-crafted visions and mission statements displayed prominently without ever achieving their stated purpose. It's what the leaders say and do publicly and privately in their places of business that matters."

I'm sure the money boys at Goldman will survive and continue to haul off dump truck loads of cash. But the erosion of public trust that began in 2008 continues to deepen, and it affects the sales force.

How proud do you think the Goldman salespeople were to have their internal conversations whipping around the world on the Internet? What if they had to give a presentation for Career Day at their kid's school? Would they be proud to talk about their employer?

If your spouse worked for Goldman, would you brag about his or her job to your neighbors? I suspect the Goldman employees probably cringed every time their phone rang the week after it happened. "Ashamed" is hardly the way you want your salespeople to feel about your organization.

Yes, profits are important; you can't serve customers without a healthy bottom line. But when you make profit your sole purpose, it's only a matter of time before customers figure you out.

The 6 Ps: Putting Profit into Perspective

Here's a framework for looking at your business that puts profit into perspective:

- Profit: financial goals and measurements
- Process: internal productivity standards and measures
- Products: innovation and product development goals
- Promotion: sales, marketing, and public relations goals and strategy
- People: employee development metrics and goals

To be successful, a business must have goals in all five areas (Figure 3.1).

There's a natural tension between each circle. Profit goals affect the goals for processes, products, people, and promotion. Product goals affect profit, process, people, and promotion, and so forth. They're all interconnected. When one pulls, the others feel a tug.

The challenge is managing the natural tension between the five areas.

The public debacle at Goldman Sachs reveals what happens when you overemphasize profit: it pulls all the other areas out of whack (Figure 3.2).

Overemphasizing profit puts people, products, promotion, and process goals at risk. A strong NSP solves this problem by acting as a central hub (Figure 3.3).

Having the NSP at the center prevents you from focusing too heavily on one area at the expense of the others. Instead of each area standing alone, they all support your NSP. We use the 6-P framework with our clients to improve organizational alignment and to ensure that no single department dominates at the expense of others.

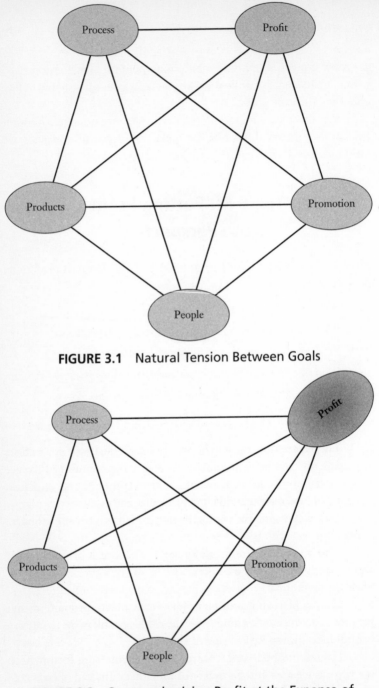

FIGURE 3.1 Natural Tension Between Goals

FIGURE 3.2 Overemphasizing Profit at the Expense of Critical Goals

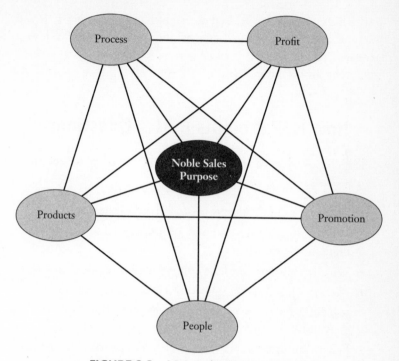

FIGURE 3.3 McLeod 6-P Framework

Without an NSP, people start to treat individual or departmental goals as the company goals. The consequences can be disastrous. The most common and ultimately fatal error is the one that Goldman Sachs made: overemphasizing profit at the expense of everything else. That's why profit isn't at the center of the 6-P wheel. Profit is a measurement of how well you are performing against your NSP. It's critical, as one of the four key areas where you set goals and targets. However, it's not the center.

Viewing the other functions through the lens of profit alone limits your thinking. Concentrating solely on profit removes your focus from the customer, stifles innovation, and distorts the entire system.

Richard (Rick) Russell, executive vice president and chief commercial officer for Sunovion Pharmaceuticals Inc., says, "It's natural for a company to focus on bottom line metrics, but those metrics must add up to a great purpose."

Working with Russell's team of leaders from multiple products lines, we crafted the following NSP: "We bring health and hope to the lives of patients." Russell describes how he uses NSP, "If you focus on profit you are focusing on the wrong thing. Profit is a derivative of the purpose. If you talk to sales reps the big wins come when they focus on the Noble Sales Purpose."

How NSP Prompts Better Questions

When you overemphasize profit, you limit yourself to questions such as these:

- How can we make our processes faster and cheaper?
- Which products are the most profitable? How can we make them more profitable?
- Which products are the least profitable? How can we change that?
- How much do our people cost? How can we generate more revenue with fewer people? How can we get each person to generate more revenue?
- What's our promotion expense? How do our sales and market-ing costs compare with the industry? How can we cut them? How can we get sales to produce more revenue? How can we get them to reduce expenses?
- How can make our people more efficient? What skills do they need to make us more profitable?

These are not bad questions. However, they don't prompt the kind of innovative customer-oriented thinking you need to differen-tiate your sales force or give you a competitive advantage.

Having an NSP at the center prompts you to ask questions such as these:

- How do our processes affect our customers? How might we improve our processes to benefit our customers? How can we be more effective to better help our customers succeed?
- What are our customers' goals? What kinds of products would help them achieve those goals?
- How do our customers do business today? How might they do business in the future? How can we help them get there?

- What problems do our customers encounter? How can we help them solve these? What products, services, delivery systems, or programs can we create to address these issues?

- In what yet to be imagined ways could we help our customers?

- How can our promotions reach more customers? How could we tailor our promotions to better serve our customers?

- How is our sales force helping our customers be more successful? How can they get better at that?

- What skills do our people need to make our customers more successful? What ideas do our people have for our customers?

- Are some customers more profitable than others? Why is that? Are we serving them better? If so, how can we duplicate that with other customers?

- Why are some customers less profitable? Are we doing too much or too little for those customers?

Can you see the difference?

The first set of questions—those centered on profits—is internally focused. They ask about your business: "How can we make more profit off what we're already doing now?" They view the other four Ps through the lens of profit alone.

The second set of questions—the NSP questions—is about *improving the customer's condition.* These questions ask how we can become more effective in each of these five areas so that we can better actualize our NSP.

Profit questions have a narrow internal focus; NSP questions open the door to a bigger, more customer-driven conversation.

The late Steve Jobs famously said, "My passion has been to build an enduring company where people were motivated to make great products. Everything else was secondary. Sure, it was great to make a profit, because that was what allowed you to make great products. But the products, not the profits, were the motivation. [Ex-CEO John] Sculley flipped these priorities to where the goal was to make money. It's a subtle difference, but it ends up meaning everything: the people you hire, who gets promoted, what you discuss in meetings."

Jobs created one of the world's most profitable organizations because he focused on creating products that made a difference in the way people live their lives.

By asking NSP questions, you start changing the narrative of your business. As Jobs pointed out, it's a subtle difference—but it's one that ends up meaning everything. NSP questions lead you to start looking in different places. They point you toward unique competitive advantages, which will ultimately wind up making you even more money.

Consider the well-known story of manufacturing conglomerate 3M. 3M's purpose is to solve problems. In fact, one of the company's engineers was so determined to solve his customer's problem that he invented a new form of masking tape, which he later developed into Scotch tape. Another engineer who was having trouble finding his place in his hymnal solved his own problem by inventing Post-it Notes.

It's doubtful that either of these highly profitable products would have come to market if 3M's purpose had been profit alone. 3M's clearly stated purpose—"solve problems"—prompted their people to start asking different questions and looking in different places for answers.

The same principle applies to sales. Sales leaders who instill a noble purpose in their teams create organizations that are constantly looking for new ways to add value to customers. They discover new opportunities. They find gaps that the competitors aren't meeting. They identify new pockets of business.

Leaders who tell their teams that profit alone is the only goal wind up with less creative, less innovative organizations. Their people don't have the internal motivation of helping the customer, so they miss opportunities. They fail to find chances for new business.

Because profit is concrete and easy to understand, it's easy for salespeople and managers to focus on it. But focusing on profit alone doesn't drive innovation, creativity, or customer loyalty. Profitability goals do not touch the human heart or move the human spirit. Focusing on profit alone will not create a sales force of true believers.

Ethics professor Pyser, who used to work as a corporate attorney, says, "As someone who has been in board meetings as a director or counsel, situations and challenges are managed at the agenda level. Anything that cannot be placed on the agenda or quantified on a spreadsheet is often perceived as unimportant and not requiring attention. With pressure to generate higher profits, ethics and soft skills are often dismissed as intangible and touchy-feely. In reality, these matters offer significant value and can be success tools to close gaps in strategy."

Pyser adds, "If you think about it, there's a line in your business reporting that says goodwill; it's always been part of accounting practices. A Noble Sales Purpose is goodwill squared."

Profit measurements in the absence of NSP shortchange your sale force because they take every conversation down to money far too quickly.

Although NSP conversations don't necessarily center on it, they certainly *include* profit. Asking questions such as, "Why are some customers more profitable than others?" or "How can we better serve our high-profit customers?" brings profit into the mix; however, it's done through the lens of the NSP.

Use the NSP questions in your next leadership meeting to start a new dialogue. You don't have to ask them all at once; just pick two or three as a jumping off point. If you're a salesperson, ask them of yourself. You may not have control over the products your company creates, but asking these questions about your own customers will ignite a different line of thinking that will compel *you* to come up with innovative ideas.

The 6-P model elevates your thinking. You can and should analyze the profit and loss statement (P&L) with a fine-tooth comb. NSP doesn't keep you from having the profit conversation; it merely adds additional high-gain elements to the mix.

Using the 6-P model with your NSP at the center helps you manage the natural and necessary tension between the other five areas. It's your True North, because it puts your customers front and center of every conversation. It resets you individually, and organizationally, and keeps you from straying.

The reason so many organizations overemphasize profit at the expense of a larger more noble purpose isn't necessarily because they're bad people. Some of the problem is greed and short-term self-interest, but not all of it. An overemphasis on profit simply happens by default in many cases, and here's why: When you look at a P&L or revenue report, the numbers are self-evident. They're concrete and easy to understand. Cut here, add here, tweak this, move that, and *voilà*—the profit number at the bottom will change.

An NSP conversation is more abstract and less cut and dried. It tends to go around in a few circles before you land on a solution. Many people are uncomfortable wading outside the sea of numbers, and this is exactly why you need to do it.

Sales isn't just about numbers. It's about real live human beings. It's about customers, salespeople, and everyone who surrounds them. The way they think and feel about one another will determine your organization's success or failure.

Jim Stengel, who drove a decade of extraordinary growth at Procter & Gamble, says, "When you take the great organizations of the world, their leaders spend their time differently. Apple, Nike, IBM, their leaders spend their time on the products, the organization, their customers and their standards. They are not spending their time managing the numbers for each quarter."

Using the 6-P model reframes your internal conversation, which will ultimately reframe the external conversation: the ones your sales force has with customers.

You completed an exercise in the last chapter where you described two things: first, your job, and then, how you made a difference to someone in a professional situation. You probably felt more passionate and enthusiastic while giving the second explanation than you did when giving the first. Using the 6-P model with your NSP at the center brings the same passion and enthusiasm to the forefront of your organization. The narrative of your business becomes about the customers, not just your own internal measurements.

Your NSP is an action-oriented cornerstone of your business. It prevents you from jumping to financial discussions too quickly by making your customers' voice a vital part of the conversation.

Focusing too intently on short-term profit is the most common cause for organizations losing their sense of purpose. But it's hardly the only one. Overemphasizing other areas such as process improvement, promotions, or even misplaced energy on products and people can a cause an organization to lose sight of its NSP. NSP may seem conceptual or fuzzy when compared with easier-to-measure things like shareholder value, turnaround time, and cost per unit. That's why you, as the sales leader, need to be proactive about bringing your NSP to the front of every discussion.

When your sales force knows that making a difference to the customers is their primary purpose, you can begin to imagine an innovative, passionate, and profitable business environment—and then bring it to life.

Do One Thing

At your next meeting, use the 6-P model with NSP at the center to double-check decisions. Ask yourself and your colleagues, Is what we're doing helping or hindering NSP?

The Sales Manager Question That Changes Everything

How will this customer be different as a result of doing business with us?

It's the question most sales managers don't ask. So the few who *do* ask it ignite a chain reaction that drives outstanding sales performance.

I know because it happened to me—only I wasn't the sales manager; I was the sales rep.

During my late 20s, I worked for a small company that sold training programs. My boss, the vice president (VP) of sales, was a man named Durwood Snead. (You can't make up a name like that.)

Durwood, an ex–Procter & Gamble (P&G) guy, had hired me away from P&G, where I'd been a sales trainer and manager. He convinced me to come to work at this small upstart training company, because he saw huge potential.

My job as an account manager was to grow the Southeast business. We were starting at ground zero. On my first day of work, I didn't get a customer list, because we didn't have any customers in my territory. Instead, Durwood and I created a prospect list, mapping out a plan for calling on the major companies in the Southeast. Then I hit the road.

During that first year, I met with Durwood once a month for a sales pipeline review. But Durwood conducted the review differently than most managers. When I brought up a customer's name, he would ask standard sales manager questions, such as, "When are you going to close?" and "Who needs to be involved?" But he'd also ask questions about them as an organization and as people. "Who are they?" and "What are their goals and challenges?" His people-oriented questions helped me see our customers as something other than a target.

Before leaving each customer, we would talk about how they'd be different if they did business with us. It was our own little fantasy about the customer's world. We'd imagine how their people would be better with their customers, close more sales, and how the managers would become better coaches. We'd become giddy discussing the ways our training programs would help their company and the people in it.

I won a million dollars' worth of new business in that first year. That equaled the amount of new business that was brought in the previous year by the combined sales force of 15 reps.

Unfortunately, Durwood left after 18 months to work elsewhere. I was promoted to VP and was given a big raise. However, I had to start reporting to the company's president.

Although I was selling the same programs and we were using the same spreadsheets for our reporting, the president never asked the kind of questions that Durwood had—about our customers' lives and ambitions and how our programs might improve their businesses.

In my conversations with the president, I found myself thinking, "When he looks at me, all he sees is a revenue number." I went from being a person who made a difference to customers to being a profit center.

Within a year, I quit.

Why Sales Managers Matter

The way managers talk to salespeople matters. It matters *a lot*.

As I look back on those conversations with Durwood 20 years later, I realize that two important things were happening:

1. We were *reminding ourselves* about the impact our programs had on customers.
2. We were *preparing me* for the conversations I'd be having with customers.

Having these discussions—about how customers' lives would be different as the result of doing business with us—gave me a different perspective on my sales activity. What you look at not only focuses your mind but translates into your behavior, which shifts people's perception and experience of you. Then the whole situation changes—all because of this gossamer thing called a thought.

Those afternoon sessions when Durwood and I enthusiastically described the impact our programs would have on our customers created powerful mental pictures I carried with me into every sales call. Instead of thinking about my sales number, or even our programs' bells and whistles, I went into my sales calls thinking about the customers: How could we make life better for them and drive results for their teams?

Try this quick exercise to see how a single question affects your mindset.

Make a list of your top five sales opportunities below or create a separate list:

Opportunity #1:

Opportunity #2:

Opportunity #3:

Opportunity #4:

Opportunity #5:

Look at each and ask, "What will it take to close this opportunity?"

As you answer this for each potential customer, monitor your thoughts and feelings. Do you feel good or anxious? Are you excited or worried you won't close? Are you thinking about all the steps and obstacles along the way?

Now, looking at that same list, ask yourself a different question: "How will this customer be different as a result of doing business with us?"

Don't give a rote answer. Really think the question through for each individual customer.

Will doing business with you get your customer better results? Will the customer be more efficient? Will he or she be happier or more successful? Will it position the customer's company better in the marketplace? How will your contact's job or life improve? Will his or her job be easier? How will it affect *that person's* end users? How will it impact his or her organization's bottom line? Will the customer make more money? Will the company save time or resources?

Then, take note of where this other-focused line of thinking takes you. Asking, "What will it take to close this sale?" prompts you to think about sales activities. Asking, "How will this customer be different as a result of doing business with us?" prompts you to think about the impact you can have on the customer's business and life.

The first question is about your revenue goals. The second question is about *actualizing* your Noble Sales Purpose (NSP). *Actualize* is defined as "to make actual: realize." Both questions are important. But which one do you think helps salespeople do a better job in front of customers?

If you said the NSP question, you're right. Here's why: traditional revenue questions prompt salespeople to think about themselves, their quota, and their tasks. The NSP question prompts salespeople to start thinking about the customer in a different way. It takes them out of a self-oriented, task mode to a customer-oriented, problem-solving, creative, and collaborative mode.

People who sell with noble purpose—the top performers—bring their NSP mindset to every aspect of the sales process. They don't merely repeat their NSP as a slogan. They make it their business to actualize it for each and every customer.

Moving from self-focus to an NSP focus is how a manager can take a salesperson's performance to a higher level. When you ask a salesperson, "How will this customer be different as a result of doing business with us?" you ignite a line of thinking that elevates his or her approach.

getAbstract chief executive officer (CEO) Michel Koopman makes this question mandatory for his sales mangers by telling them, "When asking a rep about an account during each (formal or informal) operational review, train them to expect that you will ask them one (and the same) question in addition to the usual ones (how big, when, how much, etc.) each time: 'How will this client be better because of getAbstract?'"

Koopman explains, "Making this a standard operating procedure trains every Enterprise Relationship Manager [salesperson] to think differently all the time. They eventually become prepared to answer this, because they expect their manager to ask them. If you ask it each time you talk about a client/prospect with an ERM—without any exceptions—purpose becomes the item at the forefront of their brain. Sales reps with this focus on value and purpose are more successful than those who do not have this focus."

Koopman's relentless focus on NSP keeps his sales force from straying. The leader's language is what sticks with salespeople.

How to Get Your CEO on Board with NSP[1]

1. **Lead with the business case.** CEOs are paid to deliver numbers. Use the data from the previous chapter, "Why *Profit* Is Not a Purpose," to demonstrate how NSP drives more revenue. Provide succinct information they can share with their board.

2. **Choose the right time and place.** Share the NSP concepts in a setting where the CEO can think reflectively. When Jim Stengel was CMO at Procter & Gamble, he waited until he and then-CEO A.G. Lafley were on the company jet to discuss important issues. You don't want the CEO pressured to make a quick decision or to respond in front of a group. Present NSP as idea that you'd like him or her to ponder.

[1]Created in collaboration with my colleague Jim Stengel, author of the groundbreaking book, *Grow: How Ideals Power Growth and Profit at the World's Greatest Companies.*

(*continued*)

(continued)

3. **Get respected colleagues on board.** Good CEOs get input from their whole team, not just the sales leaders. Identify the people your CEO listens to, and get their buy-in by explaining the benefits to their department. Focus on why it's a win for their function and the company as a whole, not just sales.

4. **Appeal to the CEO's noble instincts.** People often assume that CEOs only care about money. This is rarely true. CEOs want to leave a legacy. Show your CEO how he or she can deliver returns to shareholders and create an enduring company that makes a difference.

My conversations with Durwood Snead reinforced two very important points in tangible and pragmatic ways:

1. Our company makes a difference.
2. I make a difference.

Imagining how our work could improve a customer's life helped me approach my sales calls with confidence and pride. I was filled with ideas and constantly looking for opportunities, because I knew we could have a significant impact on the customers. I met with more people. I asked better questions. I was more persistent and assertive. I knew I wasn't selling a me-too generic solution; I was selling something that mattered. I had a purpose.

It may seem counterintuitive to talk about actualizing your NSP when you're concerned with revenue, but it's the most effective way to improve sales performance. However, it's hard for a salesperson to hold onto a sense of purpose without continual reinforcement. That's why you as the leader need to be proactive about bringing an NSP mindset into conversations with your team.

How NSP Helps You Close Bigger Deals

Managers are sometimes afraid to emphasize the NSP. They worry that it puts salespeople at risk of becoming service people who are too customer-focused to close. But actually, the opposite happens.

NSP-driven salespeople are great closers. They're more assertive than quota-focused salespeople, because they know that both the customer and their company benefit when they close a deal. They understand that their products and services make a difference to the customer, so they can't stand for the customer *not* to have them.

During the year I worked for Durwood Snead, I unseated a much larger competitor at several national accounts. We were a small company, yet I was able to bring in big clients such as Home Depot, Kimberly-Clark, and United Healthcare.

To say that I was a true believer is an understatement. I took a million dollars' worth of business away from our well-known competitor because I knew we could do a better job.

But it wasn't conversations about our programs that made me a true believer. It was conversations about the impact we had on customers.

It's no coincidence I left the company a year after Durwood left. Looking back, I can see why my enthusiasm waned. Even though I was making more money the second year, I wasn't nearly as emotionally engaged, because we no longer talked about the impact we had on customers. I'm sure my sales numbers would have eventually suffered had I stayed. Without a boss to reinforce the positive story about how we made a difference, I was merely another salesperson who sold stuff. It became just a job.

To be fair, my new boss may have known that we made a difference to our customers. But he didn't reinforce it with the sales force, which was a big mistake.

I wasn't the only one who quit. Most of the top performers left within two years of Durwood's departure, and revenues dropped. Within three years, the company was half the size it once was. It was eventually acquired for one-sixth of what its value was when I originally joined the company.

I don't want that to happen to you or your business. I don't want you—or any of your colleagues—to quit. I don't want you to lose your best people, and I sure as heck don't want to see your company go under due to lack of purpose.

Asking salespeople (or yourself) the NSP question—"How will this customer be different as a result of doing business with us?"— reframes your approach to customers. It's a pivot point. It's the centerpiece of an NSP coaching conversation, because it points the rep toward the customer.

And it's how you start to build a team of true believers.

A Sample NSP Coaching Session

Make it a point to ask this question ("How will this customer be different as a result of doing business with us?") whenever you do a pipeline or revenue review with your reps. Then listen carefully to how your reps answer it. Do they know how the customer might be different? Do they give a generic answer—or worse, a blank stare?

If a rep says something like, "The customer will have the benefit of our products," then dig deeper. You want your salespeople to articulate exactly *how* this customer will be different—not in a generic sense, but in real and concrete ways. Because if the rep can't explain to you how the customer will be different, then how will that rep ever explain it to the customer?

Here's how an NSP coaching conversation might play out: Imagine you're talking with a sales rep before a major sales call. The rep has been working with the customer for a while, and it's time to close the deal.

An effective coaching conversation has two parts: revenue and NSP. You'll discuss the revenue first, because that's what's at the top of the salesperson's mind. You want clarity about that before you move to the NSP portion. You handle the NSP portion last, because that's what you want the salesperson to be thinking about during the sales call. You don't want the rep focused solely on the revenue; rather, you want that rep thinking about how he or she can improve the customer's condition. Again, it's counterintuitive, but it results in better sales calls with higher close rates.

Coaching Conversation, Part 1: Revenue

Using whatever internal format or tools you use, ask the rep about the total dollar value, the close date, the competitive landscape, and so forth. Make sure the rep has clear financial goals for the account and a realistic timeline for closing it.

Next, move the conversation from revenue to customer.

Coaching Conversation, Part 2: NSP

Start with that all-important NSP question: "How will this customer be different as a result of doing business with us?"

Your role as the coach is to prompt the salesperson to think deeply about the potential impact his or her solution will have on the customer. You want the rep to identify concrete ways to actualize your NSP with this individual customer.

After you ask the pivot question, go deeper by asking questions such as these:

- How is our solution better than what the customer is doing right now?
- What impact would this have on the customer's revenue or profit margins?
- What effect will it have on *that company's* customers and employees?
- How will our solution make things more efficient, more cost-effective, safer, easier, more flexible, or more fun?
- How might this make things harder, slower, or less effective?
- What are some of the less obvious ways things will change?
- Who will be affected by this? How will their jobs be easier or harder?
- How would our competition describe the impact *their* products or services would have?

Don't be surprised if they struggle to answer these questions. Most salespeople don't naturally think this way. That's why you're coaching them.

If they don't have good answers, you'll be tempted to fill in the blanks for them. But do your best to resist this temptation, because asking questions forces the reps to think. You want their brains to explore every aspect of this. You're trying to get them to connect the dots between your solution and the customer's goals. They won't learn to think this way for themselves if you describe it for them.

If a salesperson still can't provide you with good answers after some prodding, you usually have one of two problems:

1. The salesperson hasn't internalized your NSP.
2. The salesperson doesn't know enough about this individual customer to provide concrete examples of how he or she will actualize your NSP.

Fortunately, both of these problems are solvable.

If a salesperson hasn't internalized your NSP, it may simply be due to lack of understanding. The rep may not know your products and services well enough or may not have enough industry knowledge to understand the impact that your company has on customers. The salesperson simply may need more help making the link.

You can do this by providing the rep with concrete examples of the impact you've had on other customers. (See Chapter 8 for creating NSP stories.) A word of caution here: do not describe the impact your solution will have on the rep's *specific customer.* Instead, describe the impact you've had on similar customers; then ask, "How might these issues and solutions affect *your* customer?" Describing other customers provides a jumping off point while still requiring the salesperson to think about his or her own customer in a deeper way.

The second problem—that the rep doesn't know enough about the customer to describe how that organization will be different as a result of doing business with you—is the more common scenario. The salesperson understands your NSP on a generic level but doesn't know the individual customer well enough to see how to help the customer in a meaningful way.

It's not enough for your salespeople to simply know your NSP; actualizing it requires him or her to develop more complex customer knowledge. Top-performing salespeople make the NSP come alive for each customer because they know very precisely how they add value.

It's probably worth saying something here about value propositions. It's great if you have a compelling value proposition, but don't
worry if you don't have one. Most of them are vague, fairly meaningless phrases that sound exactly the same as everyone else's—and
they're statements that do nothing to help you actualize your NSP.

Salespeople with average performance use generic value statements. They can't make their recommendations more concrete
because they lack in-depth customer information. Selling with noble
purpose requires that you link the customer's goals and your solution
in more meaningful ways.

That's where you, the sales leader, come in. When you focus
a salesperson on how that particular customer will be different, you
open the door to a new level of understanding about the customer.
This prompts the salesperson to ask better questions and make more
in-depth calls. The rep establishes more meaningful connections
between the customer's goals and his or her solution, which is how
the salesperson ultimately closes more business.

Salespeople learn quickly. When you make a practice of regularly asking your salespeople NSP questions, they begin to ask those
same questions of their customers. When they realize that you're
going to ask the same question every time you talk with them about a
customer—"How will this customer be different as a result of doing
business with us?"—they start coming prepared to answer that
question.

It all starts with a single question.

Do One Thing

Every time you review a customer with a salesperson, ask,
"How will this customer be different as a result of doing business with us?"

CHAPTER 5

How to Create
Your Own Noble
Sales Purpose

The secret of success is constancy to purpose.

—Benjamin Franklin

You've seen how organizations and individual leaders have used a Noble Sales Purpose (NSP) to drive revenue and do work that makes them proud. Now it's time for you to create your own NSP.

I'm going to walk you through the three-part process I use with clients. However, you won't necessarily end up with a three-part statement. Remember, shorter is better. The brainstorming process is divided into three parts to get you thinking in the three key areas.

A few things to watch out for before you get started:

1. **Give yourself time**. Allow yourself some creative think time. Write in the spaces, jot notes on your iPad, scribble in your calendar, daydream, and think about it on a walk or drive.

2. **Don't edit yourself as you go**. You'll be tempted to want to find the perfect words on the first try. Don't. This will cause you to miss your best ideas. This is a proven process. Just go with the flow and try to answer the questions as creatively as you can.

3. **Don't worry about supporting data—yet**. Trying to use or cite too many facts too early on will only stifle your creativity. There aren't any lawyers observing you go through this process, so don't worry about trying to express everything with data.

4. **Do it *just for you***. Don't worry about sharing this with your boss or team yet. This process is just for you. We'll cover some techniques for sharing it later.

By the end of this process, you'll have a succinct statement that is both factual and inspirational. Don't try to get it there too quickly. With that in mind, let's get started.

Part 1: How Do You Make a Difference to Your Customers?

Think about the times when customers complimented you. What did they say? Not just, "You're fabulous" (although I'm sure you are). How did they *specifically describe* the impact you had on their lives, businesses, or customers?

Here are some things that our clients have heard from their customers:

"You saved my life by recovering my data. I stopped worrying about my system."

"You helped us make our customers feel safer and happier."

"You took the headaches out of our system."

"You helped us reduce paperwork so we could focus on patients."

"You helped us reduce turnaround time."

"You gave us a competitive edge."

"You made my job easier."

So . . . what do your customers say about you?

1.

2.

3.

If you're having trouble coming up with something, ask yourself these questions:

- How do you help customers make more money?
- How do you help customers be more efficient?
- How do you reduce their stress?
- How do you help them serve their customers?
- How do you help them be safe?
- How do you improve their lives?
- Is there an end-user who benefits from what you sell?
- What impact do you have on their families?

The sky's the limit. Dig deep and think about the ripple effect you have on people.

Part 2: How Are You Different from Competitors?

How do you provide a more robust solution? How are you faster? How do you care more? How are you more attuned to details? How are you more fun to work with?

Don't use boring, company-approved jargon. Use your own words to describe what makes you different. Think about what your customers say and why you think you're better than the other guys.

We're different than the competition because we:

1.

2.

3.

4.

5.

Note: You're not going to repeat this verbatim to customers. This is an exercise to get *you* thinking, so don't worry about citing specific data points just yet.

Part 3: On Your Best Day, What Do You Love about Your Job?

Every job has good days and bad days. Think about your own position. What things do you love about it? Is it your team, your customers, your work environment? Perhaps your products are particularly exciting.

Write down the things that get you excited about your job.

The things I love about my job are:

1.

2.

3.

4.

5.

Now that you've answered the three big questions—how you make a difference to customers, how you're different from your competition, and what you love about your job—you're ready to take a first pass at creating your NSP.

What themes do you see when you look at your notes? Are there any words that jump out at you? What elements are inspiring, and which are concrete? Write down the words and themes you find the most compelling:

Words:

Themes:

Examples:

Crafting Your NSP

Your ideal NSP is both compelling and concrete. It speaks to your most noble calling as a sales organization. It should be easy to understand and repeat. It's an action-oriented statement that will inform your sales activities. Your NSP announces your intentions to the world.

Are you starting to get some ideas?

This isn't an exercise in corporate messaging. Your NSP is something that's going to drive your sales behavior.

Your NSP is a conversation starter that is designed to engage you in deeper, more meaningful dialogue with your customers. It's not a closing tool. It's an opening tool. The ideal customer response to your announcement of your NSP is, "Tell me more." To which you'll answer, "Let's talk about how we might make this happen for you."

Are you ready to write your own NSP?

Here's a summary of some examples from organizations with which we've worked:

- We help people build a better world. (Meridian Systems)
- We make transportation safer, faster, and more reliable. (Graham-White Manufacturing)

- We help small businesses be more successful. (CMIT Solutions)
- We turn employees into leaders. (getAbstract)
- We unclog the wheels of justice. (Superior Court of Orange County)
- We help people achieve financial success. (Capital G Bank)
- We bring health and hope to the lives of patients. (Sunovion Pharmaceuticals, Inc.)
- We create passionate, purpose-driven sales forces. (McLeod & More, Inc.)

You can see when looking at the sample NSPs together how each one uniquely addresses the impact that that particular organization has on its customers.

Now it's time for you for you to create your unique NSP.

Don't worry about making it perfect. You can revise it later, ideally with input from your team. In fact, we allocate the better part of a day for this process when we work with leadership teams.

If you're doing this with your team, you'll be well served to have someone else facilitate the process. This enables you, the leader, to actively participate with the team.

For the purposes of this exercise, you just want to take a first pass at it. Spend 10 minutes brainstorming five different variations before you settle on one:

NSP #1: We . . .

NSP #2:

NSP #3:

NSP #4:

NSP #5:

If you're using this book as part of one of our programs, write these in pencil. We'll ink in the final version by the end of the program.

If you're doing this on your own, sit with these examples for a week. Practice saying them to yourself and to others. Share it with your partner or a friend. Which one garners the most powerful response? Which one rolls easily off your tongue? Which one would you be excited to share with your team? Which one would you want your customers to hear?

As you start to get closer to choosing one, check yourself on the following elements:

- Is it short?
- Is it easy to understand?
- Is it concrete?
- Is it exciting?
- Could you explain it to your kids?
- Would you feel proud to share it with your neighbor?
- Does it make you want to get out of bed in the morning?
- Would you be proud for your customers to read it?

When you settle on the best one, write it down.

Do One Thing

Create your NSP.

II

How to Live by Your Noble Sales Purpose

Like water flowing from an underground spring, human creativity is the wellspring greening the desert of toil and effort, and much of what stifles us in the workplace is the immense unconscious effort on the part of individuals and organizations alike to dam its flow.
—David Whyte, *The Heart Aroused: Poetry and the Preservation of the Soul in Corporate America*

Is there anything more frustrating than trying to help your customer and encountering resistance from inside your own organization? You may want to improve life for your customer. However, *wanting* to do something and actually *doing it* are two different things.

As a sales leader, you're responsible for keeping the customer's voice at the front and center of your organization. By making a proactive shift in the way you think and talk about customers, you begin to create a new sales narrative for your organization.

In Part II, we'll look at some of the distractions and stumbling blocks that threaten to derail you from your Noble Sales Purpose (NSP). We'll look how fear can threaten your hard-won progress and how to keep it at bay. We'll explore innovative coaching techniques that will help you keep NSP alive in the hearts and minds of your colleagues, team, and customers.

We'll also look at how you can use NSP to avoid the turf wars and silos that stymie so many organizations.

Your NSP need not be confined to sales; it's a powerful tool that you, the sales leader, can use to get your entire organization pointed in the right direction.

CHAPTER
6

How Fear Flatlines Sales Calls

We must build dykes of courage to hold back the flood of fear.
—Martin Luther King, Jr.

A 1980s sales training video opened with a sales manager saying, "Sales is all about fear. The salespeople are afraid the customers won't buy, and the customers are afraid they will buy."

Sadly, the sentiment rings true in many industries. Despite their seemingly confident exteriors, most salespeople are secretly terrified that they'll fail.

If you've ever found yourself staring down the short end of a bad revenue report, you know how scary sales can be. All it takes is one bad quarter to make you start to sweat. You picture yourself huddled on the side of the interstate off-ramp holding a sign that says, "Will create PowerPoint slides for food."

Customers can feel the same way. Behind many of the toughest negotiating purchasing managers is a deep-seated fear of getting called on the carpet for making the wrong decision.

Who hasn't felt the cold clammy finger of dread? It starts in your gut and spreads like ice water through your veins, moving into your arms and legs. Your heart beats faster, your breathing becomes shallow, and you break out in a cold sweat.

This is hardly the right mindset for a successful sales call.

Some people actually believe that fear is a good motivator for salespeople. This belief, like many others we have about sales, is misguided.

Fear works in the short term. It *can* kick-start someone into action, but it's not a sustainable source of motivation. A salesperson motivated by fear will frantically fly around with lots of activity, but then one of two things happens: that person either flames out, or the activity propels him or her to some level of success. Then the fear subsides, and the rep goes back to doing what he or she always did, leaving you with mid-level performance at best.

Fear makes salespeople frantic, when they need to be focused.

The Lizard Brain

You completed the "Do One Thing" exercise in Chapter 2 where you thought about making a difference to someone. You learned about how Noble Sales Purpose (NSP) thinking ignites your brain's frontal lobes, thereby giving you access to higher-level decision making, creativity, and thought processes.

Fear does just the opposite. Fear ignites your amygdala, often referred to as the lizard brain. The lizard brain is a holdover from our more prehistoric ancestors. It has two responses: fight or flight.

Daniel Goleman, widely known as the father of emotional intelligence, coined the phrase *amygdala hijack* to describe what happens when fear ignites your lizard brain.

Goleman describes it this way[1]:

> In the brain's architecture, the amygdala is poised something
> like an alarm company where operators stand ready to send
> out emergency calls to the fire department, police, and a
> neighbor whenever a home security system signals trouble.
>   When it sounds an alarm of, say, fear, it sends out
> urgent messages to every major part of the brain: it trig-
> gers the secretion of the body's fight-or-flight hormones,
> mobilizes the centers for movement and activates the car-
> diovascular system, the muscles and the gut.

The amygdala is the most primitive part of your brain. It doesn't
have higher-level decision-making skills. It responds only to perceived threats. Unfortunately, the lizard brain isn't very smart. And
since it can't distinguish between a threat to your life and a threat to
your ego, it responds to both in the same way.

You don't make good decisions when you're afraid. You tend to
focus on the short term, and you don't come from a place of confidence.

When salespeople are afraid, they stop trying to make a difference
to the customer. All they think about is trying to alleviate their fear.

Your job as a leader is to take fear off the table. Your NSP can help
with this. It's your dike of courage to hold back the flood of fear.

Why Shared Commitment Gives You Courage

I've interviewed several combat veterans, most of whom admit to
being afraid. But there are two reasons soldiers are able conquer
their fear:

1. They have extensive training.
2. They're emotionally invested in their team.

---

[1]From Daniel Goleman, *Emotional Intelligence: 10th Anniversary Edition; Why It Can Matter More Than IQ* (New York, Bantam, 2006).

Training helps a solider remain calm in the face of chaos. He or she knows what to do, so the response is automatic. Commitment to the team is what prompts a soldier to use his or her skills in dire situations. Putting yourself in the service of a cause bigger than yourself gives you more courage than if you were just trying to do something for yourself.

In the moment of battle, it's not the fear of the drill sergeant that prompts a soldier to charge forward; it's the commitment to the team. History is filled with examples of men and women who overcame their fear and adversity on behalf of something bigger than themselves. We're stronger when know that other people are counting on us.

Thankfully, a sales career doesn't carry the same risks as battle. But it does require courage.

When you reduce fear, you enable your people to act in a bold and courageous manner, no matter how dire the circumstances. Therefore, your job as a leader is to keep the lizard brain at bay.

You can't completely eliminate fear, but you can give your people the skills to overcome it. Just like the military, you help your team conquer fear by

1. Providing extensive training.
2. Having them commit to the team.

Training enables people to act in the face of uncertainty. Reminding people that they're part of something bigger than themselves increase their commitment to the team.

Taking fear off the table doesn't mean being a softie. The best leaders set high standards. However, the standards are aimed to serve an important goal or cause.

Apple's Steve Jobs was notoriously demanding, even berating people at times. But he still attracted and retained a team of A-plus players, because they knew that he was committed to excellence on behalf of the customer.

This is an important distinction, because I don't advocate screaming at your team. But if the boss is clear about the larger purpose, true believers don't resent high standards; they appreciate them.

Fear is a given—in business and in life. But there's a big difference between being afraid of your boss and being afraid of letting your team down. When you're afraid of your boss, you go into protection mode. When you're afraid of letting your team down, you give it your all.

I know the difference well, because I've been in both situations.

A Lesson in Fear, Part 1

When I was a sales manager for Procter & Gamble (P&G) in my mid-20s, I had an experience with fear-based leadership that forever altered my perspective of sales management.

I had been with P&G for four years. I had started as a sales rep right out of college and had become a sales manager after two promotions.

By way of background, P&G is one of the most disciplined sales organizations in the world. They hire the best and have extremely high expectations and a very competitive environment. Employees are expected to deliver results from day 1—no excuses.

To call their sales training program rigorous is an understatement. During my first two years as a sales rep, my manager spent at least two days a month in the field with me, coaching and assessing every aspect of my performance. When I became a sales trainer, I regularly worked 10-hour days in the field with new reps. We'd make 12 to 15 calls a day and then end each day with a test and homework.

It's not a coincidence that many P&G sales managers are ex-military. I often tell people half jokingly that I come from the P&G "Thank you, sir, may I have another!" school of sales management. The atmosphere was demanding and competitive. Yet there is an esprit de corps that comes from being part of a high-performing team. Your boss was tough, but you knew he wanted you to succeed.

The sales leaders at P&G were relentless coaches, and I mean that in the very best sense of the words. As a sales trainer, I spent hours in the field with sales reps practicing presentations over and over again. We looked at every call plan and analyzed every number. Some of my most gratifying experiences at P&G involved taking a new college grad and turning him or her into a sales machine within 30 days. The sales leadership skills I learned there laid the foundation for my career. I'm forever grateful for my experiences at P&G—including the one I'm about to tell you about.

Six months into my tenure as a sales manager, we got a new "big boss." My boss's boss had been promoted, and his replacement was coming to town to make calls with us. To say that I was nervous was putting it mildly. He was two levels above me. I was up for a promotion, and I knew that this encounter was critical.

We were presenting a new product line to our major accounts, which included my biggest customer. My boss and I picked Mr. Big Boss up at the airport. His flight was late, so he jumped in our car at the curb and we rushed straight to my customer's office.

The customer was ready for us right away, so we had to go straight into the sales call without any time to huddle up in the lobby. I gave what I thought was a good presentation, and the customer agreed to buy most of the new items. Mr. Big Boss didn't say much afterward, but my boss, Chris, said "Great job." I thought I was okay.

After that, we headed straight for the next appointment with my boss's customer. Chris gave his presentation, which was pretty much the same as mine. His call went well. As with my call, the customer bought most of the new items. Again, Mr. Big Boss didn't say much. We drove back to our Atlanta office and parked the car in the parking deck. Just as we were about to get out of the car, Mr. Big Boss said, "Don't you want to hear my feedback?"

With me sitting in the backseat of my boss's company-issue Ford Taurus, I watched as Mr. Big Boss proceeded to tear my boss apart. He went through the presentation page by page with a scathing critique of every item.

Keep in mind; both the actual sales calls had *gone well*. Both customers agreed to take most of the new items. But Mr. Big Boss thought we should have gone for more—more SKUs, more shelf space, more advertising support.

As Mr. Big Boss ripped through my boss, I sat silently in the backseat watching as my tall, confident, smart 50-year-old boss slumped lower and lower into his seat with every word. By the time Mr. Big Boss got to the last page, my boss was a defeated man. His head was practically on the steering wheel.

Mr. Big Boss ended the conversation by tossing the carefully prepared presentations onto the floorboard, throwing a nasty look at me in the back, and stomping out of the car, saying, "I hope you two can do better next time."

As Mr. Big Boss stalked across the parking garage toward our office, you could have heard a pin drop in that Taurus. My boss sat in the driver seat, staring straight ahead. I sat in the backseat, staring at the floor.

I don't know what he was thinking. My first thought was, "I'm about to be fired."

My second thought was, "Oh my God; poor Chris. He's just been humiliated in front of a subordinate, and the only thing he could do was sit there and take it." I felt like I wanted to throw up.

To make matters even worse, while Chris and I were sitting stunned in the parking deck, Mr. Big Boss was waiting for us back in our office. One of us was going to have to take him back to the airport!

I looked at my boss; he looked at me. No one spoke. We sat in silence for a full 5 minutes. Finally, Chris said, "We better go in there." We exited the car, walking back into the office, expecting the worst.

I went to my cube. Chris walked into his office where Mr. Big Boss was waiting; they closed the door.

I suppose I could have left, since it was already after 6 PM. But loyalty to my boss kept me at my desk. If Chris wanted me to take Mr. Big Boss to the airport, I'd do it. I was a P&G sales manager. I took pride in being tough. I wasn't going to wimp out just because Mr. Big Boss had ripped us apart.

Thirty minutes later they walked out of Chris's office. Chris told me, "I'm taking him to the airport now; see you tomorrow." I can't imagine it was a very fun ride.

We didn't talk much about what had happened the next day. But two days later, the scathing memo came. Mr. Big Boss was disappointed in us on every level. His main criticism was that we should have sold our customers more items.

In retrospect, he was right. *We should have.* We had just gone for the standard. Had we talked in advance about how the extra items might benefit the customers, we could have built a strong case.

But Mr. Big Boss never once talked once about the customers. Instead he ripped through town like tornado, leaving a wake of petrified sales managers behind him. He went on to the next city and did the exact same thing there.

We kept our jobs, but he came back two months later.

Were we afraid? You better believe we were.

However, we were also ready—ready to cram every item down our customers' throats that we possibly could. We had quit thinking about our customers by that point. The only thing on our minds was how we could keep from getting in trouble.

I'm embarrassed to admit this now, but I actually prepped my customers in advance. I flat out told them, "The big boss is coming to town. Please help me out and just agree with everything I suggest when he's in the call. We can work the details out later."

I had good relationships with my customers. I'd done a good job for them in the past, so they went along with the plan.

Although I had a knot in my stomach the entire time, the day went well—everything according to script. At the end of the day, Mr. Big Boss grunted, "Much better." When the memo came after this trip, he noted my improvements.

Later when I went back to thank my customers and take them to lunch, they reduced the number of items and bought about the same number of products they usually did.

One month later Mr. Big Boss was transferred overseas. We all breathed a sigh of relief.

What are the lessons from this? If you want to make the case for fear-based leadership, you could say that Mr. Big Boss got good results. After all, we did sell more items while he was on the sales call. But when you peel back the layers to look at the actual business results, Mr. Big Boss did more harm than good.

We didn't drive any additional long-term revenue because none of the sales *stuck*. And I found out later that most of the other sales managers had done the same thing. None of the sales were sustainable, because we hadn't really made a sale at all; we'd just jerry-rigged things to please the boss.

Mr. Big Boss was right; we should have sold more items. But instead of showing the customers why it was good for them, all we could think about was why it was good for us. I was so afraid of getting fired that my customer's agenda was the last thing on my mind. I wasn't thinking about making a good business case for the products; I was just thinking, "I hope I get to keep my job."

In hindsight, Mr. Big Boss may have actually been a good guy. I have no idea what was going on in his personal or business life. For all I know, his wife had just left him, or he was on the brink of losing his own job. Fear makes people do crazy things. Whatever the reasons for the way he acted, I'm grateful for the lesson.

The Chilling Effect of Fear-Based Leadership

When salespeople are afraid of their boss's critique, they aren't focused on the customer; they're just focused on their boss. They wind up having two conversations in their head, and although one is about the customer, the other, more dominant conversation is about the boss.

Picture a salesperson at the front of a room giving a presentation with both the boss and customer watching. Prior to the call, the boss had reamed the salesperson out about performance so far this month. What do you think is going on inside that salesperson's head?

Instead of being 100 percent focused on the customer, that rep is wondering, "What does my boss think of this?" And when salespeople are afraid:

- They don't listen well.
- They think in the short term and care more about making the number today than building a sustainable business in the future.
- They get defensive when they hear objections.
- They don't think strategically.
- They're less likely to ask deeper questions.
- They become overly aggressive, which turns customers off.

And that's just what happens on the actual sales call. The detrimental effect of fear-based leadership extends far beyond that. Salespeople who are afraid of the boss wind up coaching their customers and create fake scenarios just to look good (just like I did). This ultimately affects the entire organization, setting the following chain of events in motion:

- **Sales leadership doesn't get an accurate read on the market.** The boss doesn't know what customers really think because salespeople hide all potentially negative information.

- **You waste customer goodwill by creating fake sales calls.** When the inevitable late order or mistake happens, salespeople who have already spent the customers' goodwill faking things for the boss won't have any left when they need it.

- **Customers no longer trust your company.** When customers see that salespeople are "acting" for their boss, they no longer believe that the salespeople will tell *them* the truth either.

- **Customers don't take you to senior levels.** When customers see a salesperson afraid of his or her boss, they're less likely to introduce that salesperson to *their* boss. Salespeople who are afraid of their boss lose respect and creditability.

- **Customers have a lower opinion of your company.** They realize very quickly that you are not an organization that values the truth.

- **You send a message that the boss is more important than the customers.** And unfortunately, this is a fairly common experience. Senior leaders routinely experience an altered reality when they go out in the field because their salespeople are petrified to tell—and show—them the truth.

Again, this doesn't mean you have to be a softie. You can, and *should*, demand the best from your team. I realize when reflecting back on my experience with Mr. Big Boss that he could have been just as tough and demanding. But if he had done it with an eye toward serving our customers, the sales results would have been much better. People don't take criticism as personally when they know that you're sharing it to work toward a common purpose. However, back then I was so scared I couldn't see straight.

Being afraid of your boss ignites a salesperson's lizard brain by provoking a fight-or-flight response. Salespeople who live in fear of their bosses experience reduced intellectual and emotional capacity. However, bosses who demand the best on behalf of customers have a different effect. They remind their salespeople that they're all on the same team. Commitment to the team is what gives you the courage to show up as your best self, no matter how scary the situation.

And that leads me to my second story about fear.

A Lesson in Fear, Part 2

In your 20s, a career failure or job loss can be scary. But when you're in your 40s, with a family and a mortgage, the prospect of losing your livelihood is downright terrifying. Yet that's exactly where my husband and I found ourselves in 2007 and 2008.

My husband, Bob, and I purchased a small manufacturing company in January of 2007. The company made large illuminated signs like you'd see outside of Wendy's or the Gap. Bob was coming off a 25-year career with a Fortune 200 manufacturing firm. He'd been a senior executive in both finance and sales, and he had experience in the construction industry. My consulting business was going well, but he wanted his own challenge.

In hindsight we couldn't have picked a worse time to buy a business or a worse industry to get into. The economy was within months of heading south. The sign business was dependent on new retail construction, an industry that was about to come to a screeching halt.

But we didn't know that then. Everything seemed rosy at the time.

We bought at the peak, paying top dollar. It went downhill from day 1. Within months, the construction market began to weaken. By the middle of 2007, our sales had slowed. Since there weren't many new retailers going in, there weren't many new signs needed. In late 2008, when the economy officially hit the skids, it was like someone turned off a faucet. Our sales evaporated overnight. We went from slow to nothing.

By that point, we had invested most of our cash and were deeply in debt. We stuck with it longer than we should have. But in the end, there was no saving the company. We had to let it go.

To make matters worse, I had diverted time away from my consulting practice during the two-year period when the sign company was tanking. I was trying to help my husband save it. So not only did we lose the sign company, but the sales pipeline on my consulting business suffered as well.

If you told us in early 2007 that we would be spending the next two years working like dogs only to go broke at the end, we wouldn't have believed you. But that's exactly what happened. The worst day was the day we had to tell our oldest daughter that the money we had saved for her college was gone.

On the scale of human suffering, worse tragedies have been endured. But at the time, it felt like the worst failure imaginable.

To say that I was afraid is putting it mildly. I can remember lying awake at night staring at the ceiling with my heart pounding so loudly I could barely breathe. Bob experienced the same thing.

As a parent, there's nothing worse than feeling like you let your family down. We had less than two years before our oldest daughter went to college. We'd lost one income, and the other one was down by 50 percent. Most of our savings was gone, and we were facing the worst economy since the Great Depression. With executive jobs being cut every day, we decided that the best course of action was for Bob to join me in the consulting practice.

We set a lofty goal: quadruple the revenue within two years.

I'll be honest: it wasn't hard for me to sell with noble purpose when we were financially comfortable. Putting the clients first was natural and easy. But when we were desperate for cash, there were days when my noble purpose seemed like a luxury—a pie-in-the-sky dream that I could pursue when things became more stable. I remember going into my office, staring at the big revenue goal on the whiteboard and thinking, "Right now, all I care about is the money."

It's funny how the universe likes to test people. I'd been preaching this philosophy for years, and now—with my back up against the wall—I was going to have to decide whether or not I really meant it.

Of all the crazy thoughts that went through my mind during that scary period, one of the things I kept coming back to was a random 2-second clip I once saw of Dr. Phil. He said, "Every situation calls for a hero."

I don't know why that spoke to me, but it did. I decided that I was going to be the hero. I was going to act like the kind of person I wanted our daughters to be—someone who looked fear in the face and decided to do her best anyway.

As Bob says, "You have to decide that you're not going to let a failure define you. The measure of a man is not in winning or failing; it's how you respond. You need to respond well to both."

Some days, it took everything I had to stay calm. But I knew that my family needed me to show up as my best self, and so did my clients. I couldn't run around frantically; I had to focus.

Sometimes when the stress got bad, I'd put my iPhone earbuds in and go for a run, often late at night. As I ran through the streets of my neighborhood in the dark, I'd think, "Dammit, I am going to make a difference and make money if it kills me. I don't care if I'm broke; I'm going to behave in a way that I can be proud of when I look back on this time in my life."

It worked. It was slow at first, but then it picked up steam. The more I helped my clients find their purpose, the more I rediscovered my own. As our clients became more successful, so did we.

We closed more business in one year than I had closed in the previous five. Twenty-four months after my husband joined me in the business, our daughter was accepted to her top college choice and we had the money to pay for it.

I hope that your situation is not as dire as ours was. But I'm living proof that no matter how scary this approach may seem, *it works.* It doesn't matter how badly you need the sale. When you show up determined to make a difference, you close more business than when you just focus on the money.

Why Fear Makes You Fail

We're all afraid at times. Afraid that you'll be found out, lose your job, fail—or worst of all, that your life doesn't matter.

Fear is one of the prominent emotions in business today. But it's not helpful. You don't make good decisions when you're afraid. Your personal short-term interests trump everything else. You don't care if the client benefits; you just want the sale *today.*

Salespeople who are afraid don't show up with passion. They show up only with angst. Fear-based salespeople aren't as effective as those who sell with NSP, because they are:

- Feeling frantic
- Thinking only of the short term
- Covering mistakes
- Focusing mostly on the boss

- Telling their boss what he or she wants to hear
- Resisting the unknown
- Slacking off when fear abates

However, NSP-driven salespeople:

- Are focused
- Are long-term strategists
- Fix mistakes
- Are customer-oriented
- Tell the boss what he or she needs to hear
- Manage unknowns
- Work harder in the face of adversity

When you're worried about yourself, you go into protection mode. But when the people you care about are counting on you, you pull it out of your gut to go the extra mile.

You've probably heard it before, and it's the truth: Courage isn't the absence of fear. It's the ability to act in the face of fear.

Selling with noble purpose is about taking fear off the table so that you can show up as your best self. Your NSP is about putting yourself in the service of something bigger and better than just yourself. It's about making a difference to your customers, to your family, and ultimately to the world.

Your actions and your beliefs have power. Don't underestimate the power of one person to change the trajectory of an organization.

Every situation does call for a hero. In your case, the hero is probably you.

Do One Thing

Make a pact with your team that you are not going to let fear stand in your way.

The Dirty Little Secret about Sales Training

Nothing contributes so much to tranquilize the mind as a steady purpose—a point on which the soul may fix its intellectual eye.

—Mary Shelley

Have you ever gotten a feeling about someone before that person even spoke? Chances are, you have. It's not hard to read someone's mood. Someone who is scowling or sighing heavily is likely angry or frustrated. Someone who is smiling is probably happy.

We're constantly reading each other's moods, intentions, and mindsets. Sometimes we do this consciously, but most of the time, it's done subconsciously.

Your customers read people, too. They're constantly evaluating others—especially salespeople. Customers decide very quickly whether or not someone is believable.

In a study for his book *Silent Messages* (about the implicit communications of emotions and attitude), Albert Mehrabian, professor emeritus of psychology at UCLA, asked the question, "What makes someone credible?" or "Why do we trust someone?"

Mehrabian found that the believability of someone's message was influenced 7 percent by content, 38 percent by voice tone and tempo (the way the words are said), and 55 percent by body language and facial expressions. The key issue is congruence. If someone's words disagree with his or her tone and nonverbal behavior, people will tend to believe the tonality and nonverbal behaviors.

That means when a customer is deciding whether or not a salesperson is credible, only 7 percent of the assessment comes from the salesperson's content—or the words the salesperson says. The other 93 percent is likely to be based on the salesperson's tone, tempo, facial expressions, and body language. Customers don't just evaluate the content of your message; they decide whether or not it's believable.

For example, imagine a salesperson doing a presentation for a customer. The verbal message is, "We want to help you improve your business." But the salesperson's nonverbal message is tense and anxious. The rep is pushing the contract across the desk and is positioned such that it looks like he or she is about to pounce on the customer. Which message do you think the customer is more likely to respond to, the verbal message or the nonverbal message?

Mehrabian's and other similar studies validate what we already know to be true: the salesperson's internal talk track matters.

You can approach this information in two ways as a sales leader. You can spend a lot of time and money teaching your salespeople how to alter their tone, tempo, facial expressions, and body language to make them seem credible, or you can address the root cause, which is their mindset.

Organizations spend millions of dollars teaching salespeople skills and behaviors, while paying very little attention to mindset.

This is a huge mistake.

The mindset salespeople bring into their customer interactions sets the stage for everything they do. Mindset drives behavior. It's the centerpiece for the actions salespeople take. The way you think about a situation determines your approach and directs your actions.

Customers read a salesperson's tone, tempo, facial expressions, and body language because they instinctively know that this is what will reveal that person's internal talk track.

You can say the right words, but if your mindset is one of greed, fear, or angst, the customer will know. Your internal dialogue is constantly leaking out whether you're aware of it or not. You can try to cover it with clever body language tricks, but it's a lot easier (and more honest) to just think the right thought in the first place.

Salespeople who sell with noble purpose—the top performers—don't have to worry too much about their body language or tone because when their internal thoughts leak out, it has a positive impact on the customers.

The Mindset Difference between Average and Outstanding

Most previous studies of salespeople have analyzed behavior. But behavior isn't enough. If you want to truly understand what makes someone a top performer, you have to drill down beneath the behavior to identify the mindsets that drive it.

Studying, coaching, and interviewing salespeople revealed to me that noble purpose is the overarching differentiator that drives top performers. Digging further, I identified five distinct differences between the way average salespeople approach their jobs and the mindset of the top performers.

Average Salespeople

1. Focus on the company.
2. Have a plan.
3. Want to be successful.

4. Think product, then customer.

5. Like their jobs.

Top-Performing Salespeople

1. Focus on the company *and* the customer.

2. Have a plan *and* remain flexible.

3. Want success for *everyone*.

4. Think customer, then product.

5. *Love* their job.

Think about the top-performing salespeople you've encountered as you look at the two lists. Can you see evidence of their mindset?

Now think about this from the customer's perspective. Which group of salespeople would you rather have calling on you? If 93 percent of the customer's assessment of a salesperson is based on what was read in the salesperson's tone, tempo, facial expressions, and body language, which mindsets do you think customers prefer?

The differences may seem subtle, but they're not. And they play out on every level of the sales call.

The differences in approach translate into five distinct and teachable Noble Sales Purpose (NSP) mindsets that you can use with your team. If NSP is the linchpin—the game changer that shifts your focus—then these five mindsets are the next layer.

Five NSP Mindsets That Differentiate Top Performers

- **Mindset #1: NSP reps hold two goals in their mind at the same time**. F. Scott Fitzgerald said, "The test of a first rate intelligence is the ability to hold two opposed ideas in the mind at the same time, and still retain the ability to function."

  Average salespeople go into calls focused on their own goals. Top-performing NSP salespeople approach customer interactions focused on their own and the customer's goals at the same time.

- **Mindset #2: NSP reps can sit with uncertainty**. Mediocre performers want things to go according to their script. They get anxious in the face of new information, and they frequently try to close too early and too often.

  NSP reps are more confident. They know that they'll ultimately be able to close the sale, but they're not attached to having it play out in a certain way. As such, they're better able to deal with new information and problems.

- **Mindset #3: NSP reps think customer first, then product**. Average salespeople think, "I have this product; how can I sell it to this customer?" NSP reps think, "I have this customer; how might my product or solution be helpful?" NSP reps don't start their presentations with products; instead, they begin with customer goals in mind.

- **Mindset #4: NSP reps create success for everyone**. Average sales performers tend to view other people as either obstacles to or helpers in accomplishing their goals. They often use words such as *gatekeepers, blocker, competitive threat,* or *supporters,* defining others in the context of whether they're going to help or hinder their sales efforts.

  NSP reps have a different definition of success. Other people aren't just a means to accomplish their sales goals; other people *are* their goal. They hold themselves accountable for having a positive impact on other people.

- **Mindset #5: NSP reps show up with love**. There are basically only two emotions: love and fear. They play out the same way at work as they do in our personal lives. Love expands; fear contracts. Average performers might not be quaking in their boots every minute of the day, but they spend a lot of time worrying about whether or not things will go their way. This unspoken fear creates an emotional wall between them and their customers.

  NSP reps have no such barrier. When they're with you, they're fully with you. They're passionate about their customers and their company, and they'll not be the least bit embarrassed to talk about it.

It's not just about what the NSP salespeople *do;* it's about the way they *think*. And fortunately for you, it's a method of thinking that you can learn. These five mindsets are powerful mental models that you can use to reinforce your NSP thinking with your sales force. They affect every aspect of sales behavior, and they'll help you improve your selling skills and those of your team.

Selling Skills: Art or Science?

The difference between a good salesperson and a bad salesperson is pretty easy to spot. Concrete things such as work habits, product knowledge, communication skills, and use of sales tools are all indicators of general competence. As a sales manager, you can tell when someone isn't prepared or doesn't know his or her customers and products.

Smart leaders don't waste a lot of time with poor performers. Yes, they spend a few hours trying to teach a salesperson better pre-call planning, but if the rep didn't get it the first six times, it's unlikely that person is going to improve on rounds seven and eight. Smart leaders know that eking out incremental improvement from poor performers will never drive big revenue gains. They also know that the best way to drive more revenue is to help your good performers become even better. That's where the mindsets come in.

Most salespeople are capable of selling with noble purpose. The reason they're not star performers right now isn't because they've made a personal commitment to mediocrity; it's because they haven't learned the foundational mindsets required to be a top performer.

Consider the world of professional sports. The skill differences between top performers are usually relatively minor. What sets the top of the top performers apart is their ability to master their mental game. How many times have you seen a great athlete choke at the eleventh hour? Does the athlete suddenly become less skilled? Hardly. Athletes choke because their mental game gets the best of them.

The difference between average and exceptional isn't just skill set; it's mindset. Yet most organizations make the mistake of trying to teach skills before addressing mindset. Companies spend millions of dollars teaching salespeople complex selling skills models, elaborate questioning techniques, and strategic practices. But in many cases the new skills don't stick, because the old mindsets remain.

To truly drive a team to peak performance, you have to be proactive about teaching mindset. For example, if you teach salespeople how to ask better questions, they might be able to execute the technique perfectly in the classroom. But if they don't truly believe that uncovering the customer information is valuable at a fundamental level, they won't use the questioning technique when they get back in the field.

You can't layer new skills on an old mindset and expect it to be effective. If a salesperson does not elevate his or her mindset, you've simply wasted all that money spent on training.

The Ugly Uncomfortable Truth about Sales Training

I've spent the better part of my career running sales training programs. I'm a master trainer in several popular selling skills programs, and I've conducted more than 500 workshops all over the world.

I thought I was making a big difference in people's lives over the first few years of my career. I'd spend hours helping salespeople practice techniques, and I made a conscious effort to give people my absolute undivided attention. We would practice the skills in one scenario after another. I'd work them after class or come in early if they wanted extra guidance. I wanted nothing more than to help these people be more successful.

After several years of running workshops, at the request of several clients, I began to expand my consulting practice to include field coaching. But when I started working with salespeople in the field, I had to confront an uncomfortable truth: they simply weren't using most of the skills I was teaching in the classroom—*at all*.

I remember one incident in particular. I had run a three-day selling skills program for a team of surgical supply reps. This particular program was, and still is, one of the most popular selling skills programs on the market. It includes a comprehensive sales call model and extensive questioning techniques.

All the reps demonstrated that they could execute the skills during the program. We conducted several practices using case studies drawn from their actual customers, and they all did well. These weren't generic Mickey Mouse role-plays; these were true-to-life, challenging customer situations. And the reps did great.

I went out to work with one of the salespeople in her territory the following week. This particular rep had done well in the practices. She effectively executed the call model and used the questioning technique in the appropriate ways. I was looking forward to seeing her in action.

So imagine my disappointment when it became obvious after a few sales calls that she wasn't using *any* of the skills she had learned in my program. The six-step call model? Forget using it; there was no evidence that she even *remembered* it. The four types of questions? She barely asked even *one*.

What was happening? I knew that she could do it in the classroom, so why wasn't she using it in the field? Was it her? Was it me? What was going on?

I started checking with the other field sales managers and asked whether their people were using the skills in the field. After some frank conversations and a few more painful field ride-alongs, there was no escaping the truth: the sales call models, questioning techniques, and planning tools that we were teaching in the classroom were rarely used in the field. Managers were not discussing them, and most reps were not using them.

The question was, *why?* Were the trainers ineffective? Was the program a bad fit? Did we have the wrong reps?

I have to admit, this was a painful time for me. As one of the trainers, I had spent years trying to do my best to help salespeople be more effective. Now I was being confronted with hard evidence that my work hadn't made a difference at all.

But it wasn't just my programs; it was *all* the programs. I realized this once I got my own ego out of the way and started digging.

I studied a variety of companies that were using a variety of selling skills programs.

The sad truth was almost always the same. It didn't matter whether it was a simple four-step call model or a complex multi-phased strategy program or whether the questioning technique had a fancy acronym or used basic labels like *open* and *closed*. It didn't matter who had run the program—or even which program it *was*. Time and again, salespeople would learn the skills in the classroom and forget them in the field.

It made me ill to think about the time and money that had been wasted. How many people had spent time away from their families learning skills *they never used?* How much time had been lost from the field? How many workbooks, videos, and PowerPoint handouts have been created that were now just gathering dust on shelves?

It would have been totally depressing . . . if not for the outliers.

The only exception to these findings were the top-performing NSP-driven reps. My research revealed that these outlier salespeople—top performers driven by a sense of noble purpose—were also outliers when it came to sales training, in that they were the rare group of people who actually *used* the skills in the field. They attended the same programs as their colleagues, yet whereas others forgot the techniques, the NSP reps actually applied them.

Here's why:

> Most good sales training programs teach salespeople to focus on the customer. However, the reality of the field is that salespeople are focused on the close.

Salespeople often experience somewhat of an "aha!" moment in a classroom setting. They realize that they've been far too focused on their products and that they need to pay more attention to customers' needs and goals. Since there's no pressure to make the sale in the classroom, salespeople have an open mindset—and the skills stick. But the old mindset returns when they get back into the field, and they quickly forget the skills they learned.

Average reps are usually thinking about themselves and closing the deal. Skills such as questioning and planning are quickly lost because average reps don't see a direct connection between the new skills and closing quickly.

NSP reps are different. They're able to retain sales skills, because what they're learning matches their mindset. When they learn a new questioning technique or a planning strategy, they view it through the lens of an NSP. It's a skill that will help them have an even bigger positive impact on customers. It's not a trick; it's a tool.

As Albert Einstein so wisely pointed out, "We will not solve problems with the same thinking we used when we created them."

You have to teach salespeople how to think differently in order to start acting differently if you want to create a top-tier NSP-driven sales force.

In the following sections, I've provided more detail on each of the five NSP mindsets that differentiate top performers, along with tips for using and reinforcing them with your team. Using these five NSP mindsets will improve performance and increase the effectiveness of your training investment.

You can download a PDF White Paper "5 Mindsets That Separate the Top 2%" at www.Noblesalespurpose.com/tools.

NSP Mindset #1: Hold Two Goals in Your Mind at the Same Time

Average performers approach their interactions focused exclusively on their own goals. Top-performing NSP reps are focused on their own goals *and* the customer's goals. This approach affects their sales call behavior. For example, most salespeople know that they're supposed to ask questions. Average salespeople will tell you that the purpose of questions is to uncover customers' needs. But if you listen closely to the types of questions they usually ask, you'll hear that they aren't asking questions about the customer at all. They're just fishing for quick opportunities to close the sale.

Questions such as "What are you looking for in a vendor?" or "What do you like about what you're currently using?" aren't really geared toward trying to understand the customer's agenda. They're simply meant to further the salesperson's agenda. And customers know it.

NSP reps, on the other hand, come from a place of genuine interest—and customers can feel the difference. Because they consider the customer's agenda just as important as their own, they ask more in-depth questions, such as "What are some of the biggest challenges you face in your job?" and "How do you think the changes in the economy will affect you in the coming year?"

Instead of merely trying to uncover surface needs within the small context of their products, NSP reps unearth bigger-picture customer goals within the context of the entire situation. That's why they're able to close larger sales and hold onto the business longer. NSP reps make it their business to understand the customers' real goals (versus simplistic purchase requirements) so that they can make a more compelling case for whatever they're offering.

The reason average performers can't simultaneously focus on their own and the customer's agenda at the same time *isn't* because they don't care about the customer's goals. It's because they're afraid that if they put their own agenda on pause, it will be lost. They might not be fully conscious of their own internal thought process. Yet after observing hundreds of reps, this point became obvious: average performers fail to pay full attention to their customers because they're too worried about achieving their own agenda—or, more accurately, failing to do so.

NSP reps exhibit higher-level thinking because they don't succumb to the either/or mindset that causes lesser performers to forget about the customer's goals. They hold a space for both agendas and seamlessly assimilate both sets of goals into larger, more robust solutions. The ability to hold onto two agendas at the same time takes some skill. Fortunately, it's a thought process that salespeople can learn.

Training Technique: Recast Thinking Using Visual Anchors

You can use the visual model shown in Figure 7.1 to help your salespeople elevate their thinking.

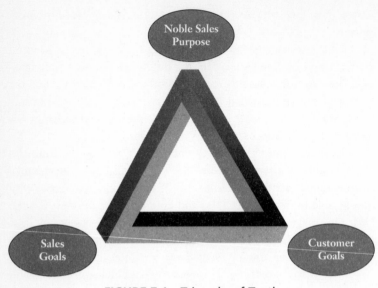

FIGURE 7.1   Triangle of Truth

This model, which I call the Triangle of Truth,[1] is easy to understand. Your goals—your truth, if you will—make up one side of the triangle. The customer's agenda (their truth) is on the other. Your purpose as a salesperson is to get to the apex, where you can actualize your NSP. Achieving this goal is built upon your agenda (my products are great; you should buy them) *and* the customer's agenda (we have goals and objectives for our own organization). Both sides are equally important and must be attended to equally.

A visual model serves several purposes. It provides your sales force with a common touchstone. It forces them to use a different part of their brains (visual processing), which opens up more creative thought. And it's an easy-to-remember, tangible cue for reframing their thinking.

---

[1] The Triangle of Truth model is used to teach leadership and conflict management. This concept is covered in detail in my previous book, *The Triangle of Truth: The Surprisingly Simple Secret to Resolving Conflicts Large and Small.*

Trying to tell a Type A rep that he or she should be a better listener and ask more questions is much like your mom or a Sunday school teacher telling you to be more kind. You know it's something that you should do, but it's hard to remember that person's advice in the heat of the moment—especially when money, or your ego, is at stake.

The Triangle of Truth model enables you to visually demonstrate a universal truth: putting your goals on pause to uncover the customer's goals doesn't make you *less* powerful; it makes you *more* powerful. Think about who's smarter—the salesperson who understands (and cares about) only his or her agenda or the salesperson who knows his or her agenda *and* the customer's—and wants to find a solution that fits both?

A visual model provides salespeople with a powerful way to solve the "my versus their agenda" quagmire. The Triangle of Truth isn't a "sales call" model; it's a thinking model that reps can use to reframe their thoughts at every stage of the sales cycle. Draw it on a piece of paper to illustrate the concept with your reps.

Being able to hold two goals in your mind at the same time (yours *and* the customer's) is a foundational mindset upon which the other four mindsets build.

NSP Mindset #2: Sit with Uncertainty

If you've ever suffered the gut-wrenching sales manager experience of watching your salesperson ignore customer cues and miss important information because they were so eager close the sale, you understand the perils of being too attached to a prescripted call plan.

Average performers actually prefer prescripted sales calls, because they get anxious in the face of new information. They try to close too early and too often.

NSP reps are more confident. They know that they'll ultimately be able to close the sale, but they're not attached to having it play out in a certain way. They are no less focused on making the sale than their counterparts; in fact, they're usually *more* focused. But they're not attached to having every interaction play out "just so."

The 1980s "ABC—Always Be Closing" cheesy old-school sales training model is not only ineffective but obnoxious. And NSP reps know this. Their ability to sit with uncertainty represents a more sophisticated approach. It's what enables them to freely explore new information rather than blowing past it in an attempt to close. This changes the feeling of their calls and allows customers to feel heard and understood; it also changes the *facts* they're able to gather. When it's time to close, NSP reps have more concrete information and can make a more compelling case.

Average salespeople often spend a lot of time dealing with objections and obstacles after they present their solution. They're uncomfortable with new information, because they're uncertain about it. They frequently ignore anything that threatens to derail their prescripted pitch when potential obstacles surface. This causes their sales cycles to flounder and stall, because as much as they try to avoid them, the obstacles remain.

NSP reps get potential obstacles on the table early. This allows them to deal with the issue proactively rather than reactively and allows them to have shorter sales cycles. They close deals faster because they're not overly attached to making the sale in the first 30 seconds.

Coaching Process: Start with the Call Plan

The secret of helping salespeople sit with uncertainty is to subtly change the way they conduct precall planning. (Note: If your people sell something that costs more than a few dollars and they *aren't* doing any precall planning, you're probably also facing the challenge of trying to turn poor performers into good ones. However, the technique still applies.)

You want to make a shift here—to help them plan not just the *end* of the call (the magic moment when the customer buys or advances the sales cycle) but also the beginning of the interaction, because this is what sets the tone and direction for the rest of the conversation. You want reps to create call openings that engage the customer in an actual dialogue versus creating call openings that simply ask permission for the salesperson to deliver a monologue.

For example, an average rep will tell you that the call objective is to close the sale. Therefore, the call opening usually sounds something like, "I'd like to ask you a few questions about your accounting (or technology, or food service, or farm equipment, or widget) needs."

This kind of opening is designed to get the customer to reveal a need so that the salesperson can pounce. It doesn't allow any room for any dialogue outside the sales rep's product area. So unless the customer contact has already decided he or she has a need, engagement is unlikely.

Rather than simply asking for permission to make a pitch, a better call opening might be, "I know that a lot of people in your industry are concerned about how the economy will affect their business in the coming year. What impact do you think it will have on you and your organization?"

When you ask average reps to plan more open-ended, customer-focused openings, they often respond with, "If I bring up something like that, who knows where the customer will go with it." To which you say, "*Exactly*. If it's in the front of the customer's mind, we need to know about it so that it can be at the front of our minds."

A good guideline for salespeople is to break their calls in half. Whether they have 6 minutes or 60, they should spend at least half of their interaction, preferably the first part, exploring the customer's situation and environment. The more comfortable they get wading through the waters of uncertainty, the more skilled they will become at identifying bigger-picture themes and pulling out relevant issues.

NSP Mindset #3: Think Customer First, Product Second

If you ask an average rep about what he or she is planning for an upcoming presentation, the response will probably be, "I'm going to talk about how this product compares to what they're currently using."

NSP reps organize their conversations around the customer's environment and goals, not the product benefits. Average reps tend to use the standard feature-benefit format. They'll say, "My widget does this, and here's how it's going to solve your problem." When NSP reps make presentations, they're more likely to say, "You told me you have this goal; let's talk about how we can accomplish it."

This reverse order flies in the face of the traditional feature-benefit or feature-advantage-benefit style of selling so many salespeople have learned over the years. It seems backward to average salespeople, who think product first, customer second. But it's not backward to the customer, who thinks goal or problem first, solution second.

Management Modeling: Reverse the Way You Serve It Up

If you want your sales force to present your offerings to their customers in a compelling way, then you need to present things to your sales force in a compelling way. Leading with your product's or service's features isn't compelling anyone outside of the inner circle.

Instead of opening your next meeting with a bells and whistles presentation about your product, try opening with a summary of the most pressing challenges facing your customers. Then explain how your new product or initiative addresses those specific challenges.

One warning: This change in order can be a challenging sell with your marketing department. People responsible for customer research are usually well acquainted with the issues and challenges that customers are facing. However, what often happens, especially in large organizations, is that the people responsible for creating sales aids and marketing materials are more feature-benefit focused. Their presentations materials can become endless diatribes extolling every single virtue anyone ever imagined the product or company could possibly possess. This spells death for a sales force.

NSP reps can translate generic feature dumps into meaningful customer connections. But average performers can't. That's why you need to do it for them.

Instead of delivering a marketing message that says, "We have great widgets! Here are the fourteen features and some benefits," you (and your marketing team) need to provide salespeople with concrete examples of how your NSP comes to life. (See Chapter 12 for examples.)

Describing problems you've solved for customers and the goals you've helped your customers achieve reinforces your NSP in a very meaningful way.

NSP Mindset #4: Create Success for *Everyone*

When average performers describe their customers, they often use words such as *gatekeepers, competitive threat,* or *supporters.* They define others in the context of whether they're going to help or hinder their sales efforts. Given that 93 percent of the customer's assessment can be based on a salesperson's mindset, this is a dangerous (not to mention belittling) way of thinking.

Top-performing NSP reps don't do that. They're more likely to know the goals of each individual they call on, including support staff. Their vision of success isn't just about themselves; it's about creating success for everyone. They live and breathe to make a difference in others' lives. So they make a proactive effort to figure out what success looks like for every person they encounter.

That's why they ask the receptionist how they can help her get the promotion she's going for, rather than just badgering her to let them in to see her boss. It's why they ask their buyer what challenges they might face in implementing the new system rather than trying to just shove it in as quickly as possible. It's why their sales encounter fewer internal road blocks and have more internal buy-in.

NSP reps know how every one of their buyers is evaluated and what their most important goals are. They also know each buyer's boss's goals and the organization's most pressing internal issues.

Leadership Lesson: Connect with Context (Constantly)

NSP reps know that creating success for others is the way you create success for yourself. The more you do it, the more it circles back to you.

It's easy to forget this universal truth in the rush of business. That's where sales leadership comes in. One of the essential jobs of a leader is to provide context, or the backstory that helps people understand the meaning behind events. Context lets people know how everything fits together.

One way to reinforce your NSP is to provide context that humanizes your customers. For example, instead of just announcing that you've made a big sale, describe the impact it had on customers. Compare these three statements:

1. **Good:** We made the sale. Yay!

2. **Better:** We made the sale and improved our customer's condition by 20 percent.

3. **Best:** We made the sale and improved our customer's condition by 20 percent, and here's how it affected one of the customer's key people . . . (followed by a description of how you improved work and life for the customer).

If the third statement includes a vivid story about how you made a difference to a customer, it will be far more memorable than either of the other two, because it reinforces the mindset "we create success for everyone."

Publically sharing stories about the impact you have on individual players inside your customer's organization creates an environment where people start to have a vested interest in the customer's success. (You'll read more about NSP stories in the next chapter.)

NSP Mindset #5: Show Up with *Love*

People get uncomfortable when you talk about love at work. We want our customers to love our products, we want the market to love our company, and we want our employees to love their jobs. Yet we rarely talk about how we as individuals can put more love into the equation.

Most businesspeople use the word *love* as a noun; it's something they want to get. NSP reps treat *love* as a verb; it's something they do. And they're not the least bit embarrassed about it. In personal interviews, NSP reps frequently said those exact words: "I love my customers."

There are many kinds of love: romantic love, love for your family, love of your country, and love of ideals. At the core, all love comes down to the same thing: caring passionately about something other than yourself.

As a businessperson you have a choice: you can show up with love, or you can allow yourself to be held back by fear.

Showing up with love is about bringing your best self into every situation. It's the difference between the teacher who is just putting in the hours and the one who is truly on fire to help you learn. One is showing up with love; the other is distracted by unspoken fears and worries.

If you want customers to love your salespeople and you want your salespeople to love their jobs, you need to be the one who starts the process.

You learned in Chapter 6 about the chilling effects of fear and how it ignites the lizard brain. Love does just the opposite. Brain science has shown that picturing something or someone you love actually resets your brain. Whether it's your spouse, your kids, or the beach, picturing something or someone you love calms you down. Your brain sends feel-good chemicals such as serotonin out to the rest of your body. Picturing something or someone you love makes you more powerful and centered.

Here's a technique to use with yourself and your reps to get in the right frame of mind before sales calls. It incorporates the NSP mindsets. Once you learn it, it takes less than 10 seconds to complete.

The 10-Second Game Changer

1. **Breathe:** This gets oxygen to your brain and more blood flowing through your body.

2. **Think:** This is about my agenda *and* the customer's agenda.

   I have a plan, *and* I'm flexible.

   These two thoughts put you in the right mindset for a successful interaction.

3. **Feel:** Envision something or someone you love.

   This ignites a positive chemical reaction in your brain. You produce more serotonin, which makes you more positive, creative, and open.

Use this technique to center yourself before you walk into a big call or important meeting. It will remind you of your larger purpose and help you bring your best self into any situation.

When I first started using this technique and had to envision something I love, I pictured a favorite photo of our two daughters. Now, I often envision my clients. Before I do a program or meeting, I think about my highest aspirations for the audience. I recall how challenging their jobs are and how much I want to them to be successful. I picture them making more money and loving their jobs at the same time. I've noticed that since I started thinking about my clients in this way, my meetings and programs start off even stronger, I get less resistance to new ideas, and people are able to embrace the concepts more quickly.

I also use this technique before important phone calls and before I walk in the door at night. It's not just customers that are reading your mindset.

It Takes Courage to Love

Showing up with love means being willing to put your heart on the line for your team. It means getting a little misty-eyed when you talk about your people. It means showing to your customers that you care enough about them to ask questions and truly listen to their answers.

Loving your customers and colleagues works just like it does with your family. You can't expect to get love back unless you're willing to put some in.

Your internal dialogue affects your external presentation. The five NSP mindsets ensure that you and your team are setting yourselves on a path for success.

As a sales leader, you play a powerful role in shaping your team's mindsets and beliefs. When you establish new mental models for your team, you start to see a shift in their behavior.

It takes guts to show up with love. It means you have to talk about emotions and bring caring into a workplace that doesn't always value it. But that's precisely why you need to do it.

As a sales leader, you set the tone. You get to decide whether you're the kind of person who brings his or her heart and soul to work—or simply someone who checks the spirit at the door and just goes through the motions of doing a job.

The truth is that you've already made this decision. After all, you wouldn't have picked up this book if you didn't care. So take a breath and decide to show up with love. It's the most powerful statement a leader can make.

Do One Thing

Print The Five Mindsets that Differentiate the Top 2% and the 10-second game changer jogger card at www .SellingwithNoblePurpose.com/tools. Carry it in your calendar and pass it out at your next meeting.

8

Creating a Powerful Sales Narrative without Sanitizing Your Stories

If history were taught in the form of stories, it would never be forgotten.

—Rudyard Kipling

Some of my favorite memories of my childhood are of my dad telling my brother and me stories about his own. My dad was a city boy from Washington, DC. Every summer, he would head down to Walhalla, South Carolina, to spend a month with his southern cousins, who took great delight in teasing the "Yankee" kid. My brother and I would beg Dad for another story about his "mean" cousins almost every night—and he was more than happy to share.

Among the most memorable was the time they told him that South Carolina bees didn't sting. The cousins walked through a bee-filled patch of clover in their bare feet, telling Dad, "South Carolina bees aren't like the bees up North; they don't have stingers down here."

My dad didn't realize that a group of boys growing up in the South in the 1940s went barefoot for most of the year. The cousins' feet were so tough and calloused that the bees' stingers could barely penetrate their skin. This wasn't the case for my dad, though. He was stung 20 times when he took off his lace-up city boy shoes to walk through the clover.

They also told my dad that putting manure in his shoes would make him grow taller. They swore that their strapping six-foot frames had been achieved by small doses of manure in the toes of their shoes. My late bloomer Dad smelled horrible for an entire summer.

Then there was the time the cousins told him that if you went down into the bottom of the well, you could see stars in the daytime. That was actually true. They lowered my dad down in the bucket, and sure enough, he could see stars in the daytime. But when he shouted for the cousins to pull him up, they ran away, leaving him yelling from the bottom of the well for over an hour until his mother heard and came to pull him up.

But our favorite stories were about the times my dad got back at the mean cousins. There was the time he went out late at night and painstakingly loosened the bolts on the front wheels of all their bicycles. The next day my dad said, "Race you down the hill." The cousins got about halfway down the hill when their front wheels started to shake and then flew off. The image of the mean cousins at the bottom of a hill in a pile of bikes as my dad rode off into the sunset never failed to get a big cheer out of my brother and me. Even though we knew how the story ended, we begged to hear it over and over again.

We also loved the one about Dad tying the mean cousins to their bunks while they slept. Then he lit a bucket of oily rags and pushed it under the bed so that they thought the house was on fire. Of course, he then played the hero and saved them.

A parent today would be horrified at those stories. But at the time, listening to those stories helped shape our self-image. They told my brother and me what kind of people we are. We weren't wimpy kids from Washington, DC. We were smart individuals who could figure things out. We were the Earle family. We wouldn't let a bunch of mean cousins get the best of us.

By telling us those stories, my dad was creating the narrative for our family. Stories are the sound track of our lives. It's not without coincidence that all the great religions of the world have a book of stories. Stories remind us of who we are and who we want to be.

The same is true for the stories you tell about your organization, whether it's around the water cooler or in meetings. They inform people's belief system and transmit your culture. They create the narrative of your organization.

Great stories inspire action. They help you reset yourself during times of adversity. Listening to stories about how others acted in similar circumstances inspires you to do the same.

To that end, stories are a great way to substantiate your Noble Sales Purpose (NSP). The stories you tell your team and customers make a lasting impression, because they touch emotions. This makes them far more memorable than product features or technical specs.

The problem is that most organizations tend to sanitize stories and boil them down to the basic facts, eliminating the very emotion that makes them so compelling. Companies use generic language such as *value, reliability, efficiency, flexibility, superior provider of end-to-end solutions,* and so on, to convey their story. But these words fall flat because they're the exact same words that everyone else uses.

Creating a New Organizational Narrative

Earlier in this book you read about Virginia-based manufacturing firm Graham-White, a company that makes air compressors and components to keep the brakes on locomotives dry. If you recall, their NSP is "We make transportation safer, faster, and more reliable."

I asked for examples of their reliability during a program with their sales force. One of their reps stood up and told the following story.

Because locomotive engines are always in service, it's a challenge to catch one to service the brakes. One of the reps was in the middle of a field modification improvement program, and he didn't want to miss the moment when the locomotive came into the shop yard. He realized that if he went back to the hotel and waited for the customer to call, he'd lose 30 minutes. Even though it was after midnight, he decided to wait it out.

So he slept in his car . . . in the snow.

The customer called his cell phone at 3 AM. Thirty seconds later, the salesman was standing in front of the customer's desk. The customer asked incredulously, "How did you get here so fast?" He replied, "I slept in my car." The customer couldn't believe it: "It's 30 degrees outside; are you crazy?"

The salesman said, "I knew you needed me to work on those brakes. I didn't want to miss it when the train came in."

The salesman thereby cemented his status as a legend: "The sales rep who sleeps in his car *in the snow* to keep the brakes safe."

This story was new information to most of the audience. The older sales guys knew it, but the new ones had never heard it before. Upon hearing it, they all stood a little taller, and you could tell they had even more pride in their company.

How would you feel about your organization if you heard that story on your first day of work? Would you be proud that you had joined the firm? Would you repeat the story to your spouse when you went home?

If you were a customer hearing that story, would you want to do business with that firm?

Graham-White says, "We make transportation, safer, faster, and more reliable." Do you believe them after reading that story? I sure do.

Stories are a concrete way to substantiate your NSP and bring it to life in a way that technical data cannot. Stories about your company do the same thing for your employees that my dad's stories did for me. They tell people who you are.

After hearing the tale of "the guy who sleeps in his car in the snow," we decided to share it with the rest of the organization. We wanted the Graham-White employees to know: we're the kind of people who sleep in our car, in the snow, to keep our customers safe.

Every business has a narrative. As a sales leader, you have the power to shape that narrative. If you want to create a new perception of your organization, then start telling new stories.

"The guy who sleeps in his car in the snow" prompted us to wonder: How many other great stories does Graham-White have? I began working with their sales leadership team to find them.

A Case Study in Storytelling

Although Graham-White's products are highly technical in nature, their impact is very human. The manufacturer's air dryers keep moisture out of the brakes on trains and heavy vehicles. Moisture causes the brakes to freeze, which makes the vehicle inoperable.

Trains do important work; they haul people and materials where they need to go. When the brakes on a train are locked out due to moisture, it causes problems for *literally* millions of people.

Graham-White's salespeople call on engineers and purchasing agents at the world's largest railroads and heavy vehicle fleets and manufacturers. Clients such as GE Transportation and Union Pacific Railroad are tough negotiators. One of Graham-White's sales challenges is that their products cost more than their competitors'. They have engineering proof that their air dryers improve safety, efficiency, and reliability better than the competitor's products. But too often, sales kept coming down to price—and Graham-White's value story got lost amidst the technical specs and contract negotiations.

I worked with their sales leadership team to craft several NSP stories. Because most of the Graham-White salespeople are engineers themselves, they focused on technical details when they first told me their stories. But after doing a little digging and tweaking, we were able to substantiate how the Graham-White products kept trains safe and on time, and in turn positively impacted millions of people. Graham-White's NSP stories are written to substantiate their NSP claim that they make transportation safer, faster, and more reliable. The value isn't in the entertainment of the story; it's in the persuasiveness of it.

To set the stage, imagine you're a buyer at General Electric or another type of big manufacturing organization. You spend your days studying technical specs and negotiating prices. You're used to reading and hearing fairly dry presentations. Every salesperson who comes in claims to be the best. Then one day, amidst a sea of vendors touting generic value propositions, in walks a rep from Graham-White who changes things up.

He tells you a story about a chilly November day when Atlanta's mass transit system almost shut down. The temperature had dropped from 55 to 25 degrees in a 4-hour period. This caused moisture in all the trains' air brakes. The moisture froze, the brakes locked up, and— right before rush hour—20 of Atlanta's trains couldn't move. There were stuck in the shop yard with their brakes locked up. It would have made rush hour a disaster and stranded thousands of commuters—but two Atlanta trains had been outfitted with Graham-White products that *didn't* freeze. The rep described what happened next:

> All of a sudden, I see all these people running around the shop yard. They're using the Graham-White–outfitted trains to physically pull all the other trains into the heated shop so that they can warm their brakes.
>
> If our air dryers had not been on those two vehicles, they wouldn't have been able to get the other trains back on the track for rush hour. If they had relied on our competitor, the entire city of Atlanta would have come to a grinding halt.

What's your reaction to Graham-White if you're a buyer hearing this story? How does this story compare to a PowerPoint presentation of technical specs and a generic claim of reliability that you heard from their competition?

Now let's take it a step further. How likely are you to repeat this story if you had to explain to your boss why you made the decision to go with Graham-White's higher-priced product?

It's very likely. In fact, that's exactly what happened. The buyer repeated the story to his boss, and Graham-White closed the deal.

Stories create the narrative for your organization. They substantiate your NSP and make your presentations more memorable and believable. Stories make your team proud.

Every member of the Graham-White sales force knows several NSP stories (see the boxes that follow for two more examples). They're not sexy stories; they're practical stories that prove their NSP. And these salespeople are skilled at telling the stories. I coached the team to help them get comfortable saying them in their own words. We created a single photo slide to go with each story. The slides have a title, such as "Keeping Canada Warm," that's exhibited over a single dramatic photo, like a mile-long coal train against a snowy mountain. The salespeople can drop these stories into their presentations with ease and continue to share stories at meetings—and the library continues to grow.

The Seven-Year Proof from Cleveland

Typically you change the filters on an air dryer every year. But when Graham-White was testing their product with the Cleveland rail system, the Cleveland maintenance guys issued a challenge: "We want to see what you're made of. We're going to see how long it can go without changing it."

The sale rep checked it every year, and after seven years, it still hadn't failed.

One day, the rep got a call from the chief maintenance officer. He said, "Who in their right mind keeps a test unit out for seven years? Are you stubborn or stupid?"

The Graham-White rep responded, "Graham-White is not stupid. But we are stubborn, because we know how reliable we are."

The customer replied, "I'm impressed. I'm changing our requirements. The new requirement for your competitors is that they have to test *their* product for seven years, maintenance free."

Guess what?

None of the competitors showed up at the bid because there was not a single competitor in the entire industry who was confident enough in their product to agree to a seven-year test.

What happened to that original product that had lasted seven years?

It disappeared off the vehicle. Rumor has it that Graham-White's competitors stole it because they wanted destroy the proof of Graham-White's reliability.

How Graham-White Kept Canada from Freezing

To say that Canadian winters are cold is an understatement. Canadians depend on coal for heating—and without coal, there is no heat.

In 2008, a railroad in Canada started buying new locomotives. Like most railroads, coal is their largest commodity. They needed the locomotives to get the coal to the power plants to generate heat.

Unfortunately, the specs on their new locomotives didn't call for sanded air dryers to keep moisture out of the brakes. They were deemed too expensive. As a result, the first winter with the new locomotives was terrible. The brakes froze all the time.

Imagine two lead locomotives pulling a mile-and-a-half-long coal train, car after car filled with expensive black coal. It's the middle of winter. Somewhere in Canada you have a power plant waiting for that coal to generate heat that will keep people from freezing to death. But the good people of Canada can't get their coal, because the locomotives' brakes are frozen. The trains are sitting in a yard in Winnipeg, unable to move.

The trains' brakes continued to lock up as the winter went on, forcing the railroad's upper management to hold lots of meetings. Everyone was tense and upset. But despite the locked brakes, the railroad still wasn't ready to make the

(continued)

(*continued*)

investment in air dryers. They asked the engineering department to come up with some stopgaps—essentially, band-aids to temporarily fix the problem. They used insulation and heat tape, standard off-the-shelf stuff.

The second winter came, and the frozen brakes continued. Their stopgaps resulted in a 10 percent improvement at best.

Finally, during the third summer, they applied the Graham-White air dryers.

Winter came along, and guess what? No moisture and no frozen brakes. No mile-and-a-half-long coal trains sitting locked out in the Winnipeg yard.

The coal trains run on time, and the good people of Canada stay warm.

Salespeople are often tempted to fill stories with technical specs. Since they spend so much of their time immersed in their products, they want to provide details. But technical specs are the opposite of what makes a good story. A good story requires some crafting.

Creating NSP Stories

Here are the components of a compelling NSP story:

- **It's true.** It must be absolutely 100 percent true.
- **It's short.** You should be able to tell the story in less than 2 minutes, which should be about 300 words or less.
- **It describes the impact on the customer.** A good NSP story doesn't stop at the event; it describes the consequences as well. For example, it's not enough to tell people "the brakes froze." Discussing the "freezing Canadians" makes it much more powerful. You want customers to think about whom the events affected and the implications for their businesses and lives.

- **It includes vivid details.** Descriptions such as "the snow was falling fast and furious, piling up around the car" or "the brakes were frozen and people were scrambling" add energy and drama to the story. Dramatic photos can make it even more powerful.

- **It touches emotions.** A good NSP story is about human beings whose lives were changed in some way. Emotional words such as *frustrated*, *angry*, *delighted*, and *thrilled* add energy to the story.

- **It supports your NSP.** The story's value and purpose is not to entertain potential customers; it is to authenticate your NSP. An NSP story is interesting to buyers who need the results you can deliver.

Every business has a story, and most of us know the famous ones: Bill Hewlett and David Packard starting HP in a garage. A 52-year-old milkshake salesman named Ray Kroc turning a hamburger stand into a franchising empire. Sam Walton transforming an Arkansas five-and-dime into a global retail giant.

The narratives of your business may not be as well known, but they're no less meaningful. As Graham-White's stories demonstrate, even air compressors can be interesting if you tell the right story about them.

What stories are buried in your business? When was a specific time that you made a difference to your customers? How about a member of your team? Ask some of the old-timers at the plant or your receptionist. People who have been around for a while are filled with stories.

As you start to collect them, write them down and share them at your meetings. A good arsenal of stories is like gold to a sales team. It reminds them that your NSP is real and inspires them to make it even stronger.

Claiming to deliver value means nothing. NSP stories prove that you do this by providing the color, light, and details that make you stand out. They remind you of who you are and who you want to be.

Stories shape your beliefs about life and work.

The Ripple of Good Intentions

At the beginning of this chapter I shared some stories about my dad and his mean cousins. In the interest of family pride, I can't leave those stories hanging as the only impression you have of my lineage. So here are a few more stories.

One of the mean cousins became a doctor. Over his 60-year career, he delivered half the population of Oconee County, South Carolina. He never made much money because he often treated people for free. He and his wife had four children of their own and then adopted a little girl when her mother, a patient of his, died. His children include a psychiatrist, a judge, and a certified public accountant. At his funeral it was a standing room crowd as person after person described Dr. Earle coming to their home, for free, in their time of need.

Another one of the mean cousins grew up to be a businessman who owned a supply house in Huntsville, Alabama. He married a girl from high school with whom he had reconnected at their 10-year reunion, after her husband had been killed in Korea. He adopted her seven-year-old son, and they went on to have two more daughters. All three of their children went to college; two have master's degrees. Half the town of Huntsville came to his funeral. His oldest daughter said, "As I looked across the crowd I thought, My Dad had a life well lived."

My dad stayed in DC. He graduated from George Washington University and went into banking. At the age of 40, he went to work for the government at the FSLIC—the Federal Savings and Loan Insurance Company—which later became the FDIC. My dad was the head of mergers and acquisitions during the savings and loan crisis of the 1980s. His job was to merge failing banks with solvent banks so that the government didn't have to bail them out. Every bank he merged was one less bank that the American taxpayers had to pay for.

He led a team of 200 people. Every Friday the leaders met in his office. He had a big flip chart in the corner of the office that said at the top: "How much money we've saved the American taxpayers." They updated it each week, and the number eventually grew into the billions.

When he came home at night, he would tell us stories—about the mergers that almost didn't happen, the team staying late crunching numbers to make it work, and testifying before Congress. He told stories about flying from place to place to keep America's financial system safe, about showing up for work with a purpose, about making a difference and doing work that makes you proud.

Stories shape the beliefs of the people who hear them. You never know what impact your stories will have on others. Good stories are like skipping a stone across a lake. It's fun to watch and fun to do—and you never know where the ripples will ultimately end up.

Do One Thing

Find three good NSP stories about your company, write them down, and share them at your next meeting. Encourage your colleagues to do the same.

9

How Sales Coaching Drives Better Customer Intelligence

As a general rule, the most successful man in life is the man who has the best information.

—Benjamin Disraeli

If you ask salespeople about their biggest obstacle in closing sales, most will say price and competition. If you ask sales managers this same question, they'll say that their salespeople lack good closing skills.

Both of these answers are inaccurate. Problems with price, competition, and closing skills are the *symptoms;* they're not the cause. In most cases, the root cause of the closing problem is *lack of customer intelligence.*

When salespeople encounter problems with pricing and competition, or they're unable to close, it's often because they haven't connected the dots for the customer. They haven't established a clear link between their solution and the customer's most compelling goals and challenges.

Selling with noble purpose requires you to develop a deeper understanding of your customers. You have to know the customer to understand how you can make a difference to that client. In that sense, telling a salesperson to become a "better closer" is putting the cart before the horse, because his or her closing skills aren't the real problem. Rather, it's that the salesperson doesn't know enough about the customer to make a compelling case.

Lack of customer knowledge is a substantial and also hidden obstacle. Most salespeople don't even realize what this shortcoming costs them. Rarely will you hear a customer say, "You don't know us well enough to close the deal." More often, they'll just tell you that they prefer the competition or claim that your price is too high. But the reason the customer prefers the competition or believes your price is too high is because you haven't demonstrated enough value.

If two salespeople have similar products and pricing, the salesperson who does a better job connecting his or her solution to meaningful customer goals will win the business. And the only way to demonstrate real value is to connect the dots between your solution and the customer's high-priority goals and challenges. This is how you actualize your Noble Sales Purpose (NSP). You must show, in concrete and meaningful ways, how this specific customer's life will be different—and *better*—as a result of doing business with you.

Of course, if you have overinflated pricing or inferior products, customer information alone will not make up for these gaps. However, if you have fair pricing and competitive products, a salesperson's ability to understand and connect with high-priority customer goals will give you a huge competitive advantage. The problem is simply that most organizations focus on the wrong information.

Five Categories of Critical Customer Information

Certain information that sales organizations have traditionally deemed important, such as data about a customer's buying history, vendor requirements, or competitive purchases, doesn't tell you anything about the customer's high-priority goals and challenges.

You can differentiate yourself and bring your NSP to life by understanding five critical categories of customer information:

1. Customer **environment**
2. Customer **goals**
3. Customer **challenges**
4. **What success looks like** for the customer
5. **What lack of success looks like** for the customer

Think of these five areas as file folders. They provide a system for organizing customer intelligence that will help your sales force do a better job of linking your solution to the issues the customer cares about.

Here are some examples of what salespeople need to know in each area:

Environment

This will help you understand how your contact relates to the organization as a whole and how the organization is positioned within the context of its marketplace. You want to know things such as:

- What's your contact's core function or role?
- What's going on in his or her organization or life?
- Who is the competition, and how do they stack up?
- What is the customer's position in its marketplace?
- What's happening politically inside the organization?

Goals

You want to find out what your contact's objectives are, as well as that of his or her department and the overall organization. The types of things you want to know are:

- What does your contact need to accomplish?
- How is your contact evaluated?
- What does the senior leadership believe is most important?
- What measurements does the customer have in place?
- Where does the customer stand with its goals to date?

Challenges

This area is where you want to find out more about problems and issues that concern both your contact and his or her boss. You want to know things such as:

- What are they worried about?
- What obstacles do they face?
- What are the competitive threats inside and outside the company?
- What resources do they have, and where do they need more?

What Success Looks Like

You'll want to know what an organizational or personal win means for this customer, specifically:

- What is your customer passionate about?
- Where does your contact hope to go?
- What does your contact's boss care about most?
- How does your contact define and measure success?
- How will your contact know when he or she has achieved success?
- How does your contact's boss define and measure success?
- How does their organization define and measure success?

What Lack of Success Looks Like

This area is where you want to find out about the potential risks your customer is facing and what the senior leadership is concerned about. You'll want to know:

- What are they afraid of?
- What will happen to the organization if they fail?
- What are the consequences for your contact?

As you scan the preceding lists, notice a few things. This information isn't about your product or solution, nor is it about your revenue pipeline or order history. It's about the customer. Product- or money-driven salespeople—average performers—tend to view customer information through the lens of their products or solutions.

NSP-driven salespeople—the top performers—take a more holistic approach. They go beyond purchase requirements and make a real effort to understand the customer's complete business environment and the goals and challenges that matter most to their organization. NSP-driven salespeople gather customer information with an eye toward what they're selling; however, they don't limit themselves to the areas that pertain directly to their products.

For example, if they're calling on a technology company, they figure out where that company is in the market and what its long-term plans are. If they're calling on a medical practice, they don't focus on one treatment or disease state; they look at the practice's clinical and financial goals. If they're calling a bakery, they make a point to understand the bakery's customer base.

Top performers know the difference between purchase requirements and true goals. An average performer will tell you that the customer's goal is to buy x product. But an NSP-driven salesperson will give you the full story about a customer or potential customer. The NSP rep knows what the customer does, what market it competes in, what its pressing issues are, who the competition is, and what challenges it faces. NSP reps understand that buying products or services is never a goal. Customers buy products and services to accomplish the goals they've set forth for their own organizations.

This broader focus enables an NSP salesperson to make strong, concrete recommendations when it's time to close. NSP-driven salespeople close bigger deals at higher margins because they connect their solutions to the customer's high-priority goals, challenges, and success factors, rather than narrowly focusing on purchase requirements.

How Information Improves Your Win Rate

Compare the difference in these two sales approaches:

Imagine two salespeople who both sell automated order-processing systems. Both systems have the potential to make the customers 20 percent more efficient.

The first salesperson has been coached to find out who the buyer is, what the budget is, and who the competition might be. After uncovering this information, the rep gives a presentation. Their presentation will most likely be organized around the salesperson's key benefit, which conveys the following message: "Our solution makes you 20 percent more efficient."

It sounds good. But it's generic. This salesperson is leaving it up to the customer to figure out how a 20 percent efficiency improvement will affect his or her organization. Average salespeople tend to use the same benefit statements with all their customers.

The second salesperson works for an NSP-driven organization, so the approach differs. This individual uncovers the same standard information about the buyer, the buying criteria, and the competition. But this rep's manager also requires that the sales rep uncover information about the customer's environment, goals, challenges, and success factors. The rep knows that the manager will ask about these things before the presentation is made. Because the salesperson is uncovering this information, the fact-finding stage of the sales process takes a bit longer than it did for the first salesperson, who just uncovered basic information. Therefore, when it's time to prepare the presentation, the NSP rep has much better customer intelligence. The NSP message connects the dots between the customer information and the salesperson's key benefit. The NSP rep uses the five categories of critical information to provide advanced context for the key message in the following way:

1. **Customer environment:** "Mr. Customer, I know you're in a competitive market where customers focus heavily on delivery times."
2. **Customer goals:** "You told me your primary objective is growing market share."
3. **Customer challenge:** "Slow turnaround time is costing you customers."
4. **What success looks like:** "Improving efficiency by 20 percent will give you a competitive advantage that will help you grow share."
5. **What lack of success looks like:** "If you can't improve efficiency you're likely to lose customers."

The NSP rep then delivers the message: "Our solution will help you win customers because your system will be 20 percent more efficient."

Which one of these messages would you rather present to the chief financial officer (CFO) if you were the buyer? The first one, who speaks in general terms about efficiency, or the second one, who directly links to your high-priority goals and challenges?

Think about one of your upcoming presentations. Look at each of the five prompts and identify what you'd say in each area. How can you do a better job of linking your solution to the critical customer information?

The difference between the preceding two presentations isn't in product or benefits. The difference is in the customer information.

The first presentation is generic because the salesperson didn't uncover enough relevant customer information to make a compelling case for the proposed solution. However, the second presentation—for the exact same product—describes the impact the solution will have on this specific customer. The reason the salesperson is able to give a more compelling message isn't because of better presentation *skills*. The NSP salesperson simply did a more thorough job during the fact-finding calls. The NSP rep knows the customer's environment, goals, challenges, and success factors, making it possible to present a more concrete case.

And the reason the NSP salesperson did a better job in fact-finding isn't because a manager said, "Ask better questions" or "Be a better closer." It's because the manager asked about the five categories of customer information.

Are you getting a sense of what's happening here? The key difference is the customer information. The reason the first rep, or average rep, didn't uncover the information is because the focus was on the product. A manager didn't provide a blueprint for gathering the customer information that would enable the rep to stand out from the competition. The NSP salesperson only *appears* to have better presentation skills. In reality, however, it was the information gathering that enabled the rep to create a better message. And the rep gathered better information because a sales manager required it, whereas the generic rep's manager didn't.

When a manager focuses exclusively on customer order history, contact information, and buying patterns, the salesperson is much less likely to gather the customer intelligence needed to make a compelling presentation. But when the manager focuses on true *customer intelligence*—the customer's environment, goals, challenges, what success looks like, and what lack of success look like—the salesperson is prompted to look for that information during the fact-finding stage of the sales process.

Top-performing NSP-driven salespeople proactively seek customer information in all five categories because they know you can't make a difference to your customers if you don't *understand* them. You can't connect the dots to customer goals and challenges unless you know exactly what those goals and challenges are.

It all starts with the information, specifically, the five categories mentioned previously. These apply to many areas within a given customer situation. Of course, you likely wouldn't be able ask about *all* of these areas in a single sales call. A salesperson may have to make multiple calls to multiple people to get a full picture of the customer. The five categories of critical customer information are a system to help salespeople gather the right customer intelligence. A salesperson who is ready to close a deal should have a good handle on all five areas.

The sale is at risk if a salesperson doesn't have this information. Without a solid understanding of the customer's environment, goals, challenges, and success factors, salespeople wind up giving generic presentations and proposals. They can't provide concrete descriptions of how the customer will be different because they don't have a thorough understanding of where the customer is today or where the customer wants to go. This lack of connection to any meaningful customer goals renders salespeople unable to differentiate themselves. And in the absence of competitive differentiation, customers make decisions based on price.

Some salespeople argue that they don't have time to gather this kind of customer intelligence. The people who make these claims tend to be mid-level performers. Field observation of top-performing salespeople revealed that they spend more time than average performers in the fact-finding stage of the sales cycle, which, in turn, increased their close rate and shortened their sales cycle. It's not endless time, because top-performing NSP reps ask efficient questions that uncover valuable information. And the time they spend gathering this information pays off at the end of the sales cycle. There's less back and forth negotiation about price, and large deals are approved faster.

You learned in a previous chapter that asking a salesperson, "How will this customer be different as a result of doing business with us?" ignites a new line of thinking. Asking your sales staff about the five critical categories of customer information takes this thinking to the next level.

Use the five critical areas as prompts to help you identify where there are gaps in a salesperson's knowledge about the customer. Think of these categories as a jumping off point to help you figure out what information the salesperson needs to uncover *before* trying to close the deal.

It's best to start by identifying the information gaps and then come up with the questions you need to ask the customer. It's important to complete this two-step process in this order: identifying information gaps and *then* crafting the appropriate questions. I've found in working with reps and managers that those who jump straight to creating questions miss critical customer information. If you consider all five categories first, you're in much better shape to create a questioning strategy, because you know what and where the information gaps are.

Following are 10 great questions to ask customers. Notice that each includes a spot for you to fill in the information you're seeking. Once you know what you're looking for, you can use the questions as a template. Keep in mind that the word order in the questions is important. Their format was created after observing which type of questions got the best response from customers.

---

10 Great Questions to Ask Your Customers

Great questions are sincere, are well planned, and zero in on the customer's environment, goals, challenges, and success factors:

1. What do you enjoy most about (insert important job activity)?

    Asking someone to describe the best part of his or her job sets a positive tone and opens a window into that person's world.

2. What's the most challenging part of (something about the person's role or function)?

    This demonstrates that you're genuinely interested in what it's like to live in his or her world.

3. If you could change anything about (a current pressing situation), what would it be?

    This helps you understand your contact's goals and challenges. Warning: You want to be sure to ask this in a nonmanipulative way. You're not fishing; you're interested.

4. How is this (change, event, or situation) affecting you?

    The tendency is to ask, "What do you think about this?" But asking how something *affects* a person gets you a much deeper, more meaningful response.

5. When you look at X (challenge) and Y (other challenge), how do you prioritize between the two?

    This prompts inner reflection, which, in turn, gives you clues about the customer's thought process and lets you uncover what's really important to him or her.

    (continued)

(continued)

6. How do *you* feel about this (key initiative or goal in the customer's organization)?

   This demonstrates that you're interested in your customer's perspective, not just making the sale.

7. What do you think is causing (situation that's on his or her mind)?

   This prompts you customer to think about root causes, which will enable you to connect the dots—and discover what issues are likely most important to senior leadership.

8. How can I best support you on (big project, goal, or challenge)?

   This enables your contact to define what he or she really wants, and it tees you up to provide specific, requested help.

9. What is your deepest fear about (something important to your customer)?

   This allows your contact to share an area of vulnerability, which, contrary to popular belief, most people actually *like* to do, as long as the listener makes it safe.

10. What are your highest hopes for (your job, company, or project)?

    When someone shares his or her hopes with you, that person is telling you what really matters to him or her and giving you a chance to join the team.

You learned in Chapter 7 that customers are constantly reading your mindset. It's important to remember this when you're asking them questions, because customers can tell if you're coming from a place of genuine interest. If you're just trying to check the box in order to close, customers will sense this—and won't reveal as much information.

Don't be surprised or frustrated if it's a bit slow going when you're asking your salespeople about the five categories. Most salespeople don't think about their customers in this way, and that's why they're not top performers—yet.

If a salesperson answers with product-focused answers (as opposed to true customer information), then push harder. You want your salespeople to take off their product lens and look more holistically at the customer. When salespeople know that you, the leader, are always going to ask about the customer's environment, goals, and challenges, they will in turn begin seeking that very information on their sales calls. When they're aware that you expect them to understand what success and lack of success looks like for each customer, they will come prepared to describe that.

In this way, the questions you ask your salespeople become the questions they ask their customers. If you want to differentiate yourself, you need to know a lot more about customers than just their name, address, and order history. An NSP-driven salesperson's ability to understand and connect with the customer's high-priority goals and challenges is what sets him or her apart from the competition. The right information helps you close sales faster and keeps you out of price wars.

Capturing the right customer information also helps the rest of your organization. When you have accurate information about your customer's goals and challenges, you can share it with your marketing and product development teams. Your salespeople are the conduit to the customer. Sharing the information that salespeople capture about customers broadly gives everyone in your organization better insights into your customers' world.

You can't partner with people you don't understand. Understanding customers on a deep level makes salespeople more empathetic and more assertive at the same time. When you know exactly how the customer will benefit, you have more urgency about closing the deal.

The information you track about customers tells your salespeople what's important.

Do One Thing

Before important presentations, ask your salespeople about the customer's environment, goals, and challenges. Have them describe what success and lack of success looks like for their customer. If they can't do it, they're not ready to close.

10

How to Keep Your Sales Force from Being Sabotaged by Your CRM

*If we continue to develop our technology without wisdom or prudence,
our servant may prove to be our executioner.*
                                        —General Omar Nelson Bradley

What do you do when you walk into your office? If you're like most people, you turn on your computer and respond to the information that presents itself on the screen.

What you see on your computer screen *matters*, because it directs the course of your day. If you started in sales prior to 1990, you started your day with a customer list, a map, and some call plans. But anyone working in sales today starts off on the computer.

Several years ago, I began working with a major manufacturing firm that had recently implemented a new customer relationship management (CRM) system with all the bells and whistles. Reps could enter customer data from their smartphones, iPads, or laptops. Managers could cross-reference and analyze the data in a million different ways. Senior leadership and marketing could use the customer intelligence for strategic planning.

But there was just one problem: the expensive new system hadn't improved the close rate one bit. So they brought me in to help them figure out why. The answer became obvious to me after I spent time in the field with the company's top reps: the system captured the information that mattered to the *company*. But nowhere was there a space to record the information that mattered to the *customer*.

The top rep described it this way: "It tracks every piece of data you could ever want. But I have to create an attachment for the information that [actually] helps me *sell*. I can put call notes in the open notes section, but I'd have to go back and read the notes for each individual call. If a customer tells me his goals, I need a place to put that on my main screen. I don't want to have to dig back through 10 screens of call notes. Why isn't there a place on the main screen to write down the things that the customer cares about?"

There was no designated place to capture information about the customer's environment, goals, or challenges. There wasn't a single screen or even a box to record the critical customer information that should be the centerpiece of every sales call. And this, of course, was a huge problem.

How CRM Affects Sales Calls

The information in a company's CRM system has a bigger impact on selling skills than most organizations realize. Compare and contrast the following two scenarios:

Two competing salespeople are calling on the same customer. Salesperson A is making his call at 10 AM, and Salesperson B is making her call at 11 AM.

They both do the exact same thing before they go into their respective calls: they open their laptops to quickly review the customer's information. As they scroll down past the customer contact info, the two salespeople see two different things.

Salesperson A sees a revenue pipeline and order history.

Salesperson B sees five boxes:

1. Environment
2. Goals
3. Challenges
4. What success looks like
5. What lack of success looks like

Each box contains a succinct summary of the information they've gathered on previous sales calls.

Which salesperson is going to make the better call? Who is going to open with something of interest to the customer? Who is going to ask better questions? Who is better prepared to discuss the customer's most pertinent business issues? Who is going to do a better job of aligning the solution with the customer's key goals?

Now take it to the next level. If you were the customer, which screen would you rather have a salesperson looking at before making a sales call on *you?*

The answer is obvious, of course; Salesperson B is going to be better prepared because she's going into the sales call thinking about the customer. If the two salespeople's products and pricing are about the same, Salesperson B will beat Salesperson A every time. In fact, I'll take this a step further. Even if Salesperson B is selling a higher-priced product, she will still win the business. And here's why:

Salesperson A's CRM system set him up to make a product-focused sales call. The last thing the rep saw before he went into the call was a pipeline projection. Without being prompted to focus on the customer's goals and challenges, Salesperson A will do what most average-performing salespeople do: provide a generic description of his products and services.

Salesperson B's CRM system set her up to make a customer-focused sales call. Because it put information about the customer's environment, goals, challenges, and success factors up front, those are the last things she thought about before going into her call. And the last thing she thinks about before walking in determines the first thing she'll say when she gets there. As such, Salesperson B is much more apt to open her sales call by focusing on the customer's goals, because this is the information she's just seen on her computer. This customer-focused mindset will likely play out in every aspect of Salesperson B's sales call. She will be better able to connect the dots between the customer's high-priority goals and her solution, because her system set her up to do just that.

Why Computer Screens Are More Powerful Than Sales Managers

What percentage of sales calls does a salesperson make with his or her manager? Is it 2 percent, 10 percent, or 20 percent?

For what percentage of sales calls does a rep get precall or postcall coaching from a manager? On 20 percent, 30 percent, or 40 percent?

For what percentage of sales calls does a rep use CRM?

Probably 100 percent.

Like it or not, your CRM has a bigger presence on sales calls than the manager. Although it's scary to think that technology has a more significant impact on your salespeople than their boss does, this is reality. Salespeople spend much more time with their computers than with their managers.

In the previous chapter, you learned why and how to require more robust customer information to compel better sales call behavior. Now I'd like you to consider what happens when the technology doesn't support Noble Sales Purpose (NSP) coaching.

If you're coaching salespeople to capture more information about customers' environments, goals, challenges, and success factors—but don't give them a clear place to record this information—they're not very likely to remember or value these data. Whatever information the screen requests will be the information that dominates.

The computer screens that your salespeople see determine how they act. That's why you need to pay careful attention to what you're putting in front of them.

Analytics versus Sales Call Behavior

Organizations invest in CRM systems to capture better information—which, in theory, should help you drive more revenue. However, these systems often encourage a need for internal analytics that impact what actually happens in the field. And this can have a detrimental effect on sales calls.

CRM expert and strategic consultant Chris Meyer, who works with clients such as McKesson, Lowe's, and United Healthcare, says, "A lot of senior sales executives fall into the trap of [completing] reports for reports' sake. A large part of any senior manager's business life is spent in meetings—either defending, justifying, or celebrating his or her successes. The information they share comes from reports and the data that drives those reports. Often what you find is that instead of building a CRM for their salespeople, senior leaders will [claim to] need a system that will help [them] in the board room."

Meyer continues, "It's not necessarily a system that will help Joe Salesrep sell more; it's one that will help me, the leader, with my PowerPoints because I'm not getting the numbers out of the system I need."

Think about the kinds of information that your own CRM system captures. Is there anywhere to include information about customers' environments, goals, challenges, and success factors?

A successful CRM tool delivers useful analytics and reports. But don't make the mistake of letting the tail wag the dog.

If you already have a robust CRM and you're not capturing information about customers' environments, goals, challenges, and success factors, it's usually a simple fix; just change a few of the fields. In working with clients, we've found that a few critical tweaks to the customer profile screens can have a major impact on sales call behavior.

Our experience has shown what you have no doubt experienced yourself:

- Sales training with no reinforcement results in 90 percent of new behavior being lost in 30 days.
- Sales training with ongoing sales coaching results in 50 percent of new behavior being retained, on average; however, this varies wildly depending on the coaches' skill.
- Sales training with ongoing coaching plus daily CRM reinforcement prompts new behaviors to become embedded in the company culture.

American Society of Training and Development (ASTD) studies validate this. If you've been in sales leadership for any length of time, you've probably seen plenty of flash-in-the-pan training programs that no one remembered the following week. This is why we make sure the technology is supporting the new behaviors whenever we implement sales programs with clients. Otherwise, we know it's just a waste of money.

The ultimate purpose of capturing customer information is to *drive more sales.* Whether you do it electronically or manually, the information you require your salespeople to gather about their customers will influence their sales behavior.

If you want each salesperson to discuss the customer's environment, goals, challenges, and success factors on sales calls, you need to ask about those things in your coaching sessions—and you need to include them in your CRM.

You can be a me-too sales force that says they want to make a difference to customers, or you can be the rare company that *actually does it.* Capturing the right information about your customers helps you put your good intentions into action.

Do One Thing

Make sure your CRM has a place to capture information about customers' environments, goals, challenges, and success factors. If it currently doesn't, revamp it so that it does.

11

The Trojan Horse

Using Case Studies to Grab New Markets

I'm a great believer that any tool that enhances communication has profound effects in terms of how people can learn from each other.

—Bill Gates

Capturing the right information about customers drives revenue. Capturing the right information about sales success can drive revenue through the roof.

Former Citrix chief strategist Traver Gruen-Kennedy describes how this company's sales force used case studies to drive revenue from $0 to $500 million between 1995 and 2000.

Citrix was an early champion of cloud computing. Although this is part of Internet lexicon now, not many people were familiar with this notion when Citrix was getting started. As Gruen-Kennedy says, "We had a product at the beginning, but we didn't have a lot of sales. We were trying to learn where [we could] bring a lot of value. Some industries and professions are very quick to transition, and others are laggards. We were [looking for] a niche that we could replicate. [We knew that if] we found it, we'd want to articulate it to everyone in our sales organization."

Gruen-Kennedy continues, "We had a growing national and international sales force. [So we figured that] if every person wrote up one of their sales wins and we shared it with them in sales meetings, we could have build on those early wins."

So every month, every salesperson wrote up a case study. As Gruen-Kennedy explains, "We used a one-page template. It allowed them to do it very quickly, [since] you only had to do one a month. Usually you were bragging about your big win, which gave salespeople a way to highlight their success. They were very widely circulated, [allowing] them to get attention about their specific win."

This system validated and publically acknowledged the salespeople; however, it also did something else. It socialized the information. It gave the sales force concrete examples of how they actualized their NSP. It took the concept of storytelling one step further. The one-page documents included why the customer chose Citrix, the value story, the things that made a difference, and the impact the sale had on the customer.

Gruen-Kennedy says, "One of the places we had an early win was the mobile industry in Canada. We sold them the technology to host their applications. The moment that [this] happened, we were then able to articulate its value and the needs analysis through these case studies. [This allowed us to] then replicate that across the whole mobile industry."

According to Gruen-Kennedy, the secret is: "Keep it simple. The case studies should be a data driven and part of the sales force's normal reporting cycle."

Celebrating versus Sharing

Imagine what would have happened if Citrix had done what most companies do. A rep closes a big deal in a new industry. He might get a bonus, the president might announce it at a meeting, and he may even be asked to share the secret of his success at a training session. But what happens to the knowledge? It's appreciated, but it's not *shared*.

Imagine you're another sales rep at the annual meeting, and you hear about Joe's big sale into the mobile industry. Are you going to go up to Joe afterward and ask how he did it? Are you going to write down all the things he said contributed to his success? Are you going to ask about the buyer's most pressing issues or what's going on in that industry?

Probably not. You'll likely buy Joe a drink at the bar and make a silent vow to beat him out next year.

But now imagine you're a Citrix salesperson. At the end of each month, you get a library of short case studies describing how your peers closed business in various industries. Oh look, there's one about food service; you have a food service customer on your prospect list. Hmm, someone sold something to a division of Ford. You have a Ford division in your territory. The case study says that the buyer needed a way to organize people globally; the division in your territory serves global customers. Hmm, that might be a good way to open a sales call.

Are you getting what's happening here?

The salespeople used the case studies to go after similar business. The case studies both motivate and inform them. They can take a salesperson from merely envying top rep Joe to learning from him. When salespeople have a library of case studies, they have the best sales information in the world at their fingertips.

We've already emphasized how crucial it is to use stories to substantiate your NSP and describe how you made a difference to customers. NSP case studies, like those that Citrix uses, take it even further, because they describe how the salesperson *actualized* the NSP.

Gruen-Kennedy says, "If you have one sentence in that case study that says what made the difference between success and failure with this company, it allows the other salespeople to be creative. We don't think of salespeople as creative, but they need to be."

Gruen-Kennedy continues, "Something amazing starts happening as a result of using these case studies: when salespeople see them, they start to see the value they provide. One of the first things they do is start calling each other—and you have one successful salesperson talking to another successful person. It reinforces the tribal nature, which is a very good thing."

"If you're in France and are prospecting or looking for information, wondering, 'Who could I be calling on?' you go back and look at the repository. You look to see what's in all the case studies in insurance or automotive."

This system became a real resource for new members of the company to see what was happening.

The Trojan Horse of Sales

Gruen-Kennedy describes why the case studies mattered so much: "This was the early days of CRM [customer relationship management], [so] there was a tendency to want to move toward all of that data. The data that come from those types of systems are helpful; you can track how you are touching people, when you touched them, etc. But the case study repository got more to the meat of it."

Gruen-Kennedy explains why they circulated the case studies broadly through the company: "It's a way of validating customer wins and keeping sales, marketing and product development connected to the customer."

He says, "It was like a Trojan horse. Once you opened it, you could go everywhere."

The Trojan horse won.

Citrix drove the revenue to $500 million in five years. By 2005, the company had broken $1 billion in annual revenue, making it one of the world's largest software companies. Every rep continued to do one case study a month.

After 9 years, Gruen-Kennedy left Citrix to pursue his goal of clean energy. He now serves as the chairman and chief executive officer of Molecular Power Systems, an emerging leader in clean fuel. The World Economic Forum named Gruen-Kennedy a Technology Pioneer for his contributions to technology and to society.

He still swears by the case studies; in fact, he helped us create a template that you can download for free by going to www.NobleSalesPurpose.com/tools.

If you're trying to capture new markets, NSP case studies can be your Trojan horse. When your salespeople open them, they have an army of success behind them.

Do One Thing

Download the case study template at www.NobleSalesPurpose.com and ask your reps to fill it out once a month. (Thanks to Traver Gruen-Kennedy for helping us create this.)

12

How to Keep Your Noble Sales Purpose from Being a Mere Tagline

Any fool can write a bad ad, but that it takes a real genius to keep his hands off a good one.

—Leo Burnett, Advertising's original "Ad Man"

Marketers appreciate the value of a great message. So the right Noble Sales Purpose (NSP) can make a marketer's heart sing. But ironically enough, the very people who appreciate the value of a meaningful message often unintentionally undermine it.

Marketing's temptation is to turn your NSP into a tagline, since good marketers are always eager to share a great brand message.

A compelling NSP fills the bill. It's the perfect tagline to put on your website and to include in your literature and ads.

Unfortunately, the marketing team often takes it one step too far by using the NSP to create scripts for sales calls. This is certain death for a sales force.

It seems logical when you look at it from a marketer's perspective. Your NSP is concrete and meaningful; why *wouldn't* you want to lead with it on sales calls?

Because what works in marketing doesn't work in sales.

Leading with your NSP on sales calls *prevents* you from actualizing it. As you know from what you've already read, generic NSP presentations run the risk of failing to engage individual customers.

Think about it this way: if marketing is a résumé, then sales is the job interview. You use your résumé to talk about yourself and provide a one-way push of information. However, during the job interview, you ask questions about the employer—*then* you talk about how you can help the company achieve the goals shared with you.

Marketing uses the NSP to attract customers in the same way that you use a résumé to attract potential employers. But it's the salesperson's—that is, the interview's—job to identify how it applies to each individual customer (or how you fit into a particular company).

Organizations make four common mistakes with regard to marketing and sales integration:

1. Treating sales calls like commercials
2. Failing to flip the switch in the handoff from marketing to sales
3. Creating marketing messages for "ideal" customers instead of actual customers
4. Creating marketing materials that don't match the sales cycle

If you're the vice president of sales *and* marketing, this chapter will help you improve the integration between the two functions. The more clarity you have about the differences between these two disciplines, the more powerful each group can become.

If you're a sales leader who doesn't have marketing responsibilities, this chapter will show you how you can get better support from your internal marketing team. Here's a close look at the four common mistakes and how to avoid them.

Mistake #1: Assuming That Sales Calls Are Commercials

There's a point in every sales cycle where marketing ends and sales starts. Although people often lump sales and marketing together as if they're same thing, they're not.

Moving from marketing into sales mode requires a shift in mindset and behavior. It's almost like flipping a switch. Not understanding this critical difference is fatal to a sales force. Let's look at an example.

Imagine a pharmaceutical company sells a drug that treats a variety of conditions. They have a clinically proven competitive advantage. Their drug is just as effective as their competitor's, but it has fewer side effects.

After researching the target market—physicians and patients—the marketing department settles on a core message: "We heal patients with no painful side effects." They create a campaign that includes sales tools, brochures, and presentations.

Up until this point, everything is great. But here's where the trouble starts. When it's time to move from marketing mode to sales mode, no one flips the switch or changes behavior or mindset.

The marketing department *should* teach the sales force why the message matters. They *should* help the salespeople figure out how to connect the dots to their individual customers' goals and challenges. But instead, they simply hand the sales force a script that they're told to use with every account to ensure a consistent message. The salespeople practice delivering the message, and they do it the same way every time. They become so good at it, they sound just like a commercial.

And that is where the problem lies. Customers *hate* commercials.

Sales calls aren't meant to be commercials; they're meant to be an interpersonal interaction between two human beings. The minute a salesperson starts sounding like a prescripted commercial, customers turn them off.

Unfortunately, the previous example isn't fiction. It's real—and it happens every day in lots of companies.

It's tempting to want to script your salespeople when you have a powerful message. But it never works.

In the previous example, the marketing department's research proved that "having no side effects" is a powerful benefit. But repeating it to the customer at the beginning of a sales call doesn't make it powerful. The best way to make it powerful is to discover the impact that side effects are having on the patient and the practice. Does it cause problems for the nurses or the doctors? How does it affect their ability to treat the patient? Do they have to spend extra time? Does it prevent the patient from taking the medication?

A salesperson who knows this information can make the benefit come alive. Without it, however, he or she is just another generic salesperson reading off a marketing brochure.

Market research is extremely helpful for salespeople. Knowing what most customers care about can guide your questioning. But assuming that you know *before* they've told you does you more harm than good as a salesperson.

Compare and contrast these two statements:

Statement 1, Organized around the *Market Research:*

"Our research reveals that 85 percent of doctors worry about side effects. Do you agree this is important? Let's talk about how we eliminate these."

Statement 2, Organized around the *Customer's Challenge:*

"Your nurse told me that you were having problems with side effects. Can we talk about how side effects are affecting your patients and staff?"

Do you see the difference? Statement 1 assumes this customer is just like every other customer. Statement 2 addresses an issue that is specific to this customer (that the rep uncovered on a previous call). In this case, the salesperson knew to look for the issue (side effects) because the market research told the rep it was likely there. But the salesperson validated it with someone in the customer's office first, then discussed how it related to that specific customer.

The salesperson's understanding of an issue should guide what fact-finding questions are asked. However, customers don't believe that a salesperson truly understands their goals and challenges until they (the customers) share that information themselves.

When a salesperson tells customers what they should be concerned about, they may or may not listen. It's very likely that the salesperson's words will go in one ear and out the other, especially if the customer is busy. But if a customer tells the sales rep what he or she is concerned about—and then the rep offers to help—the customer will pay close attention to what the rep is saying.

This is why marketing-driven scripts don't work in sales. You can provide salespeople with nuggets of information to share and with market research so that they know what questions to ask. You can even provide them with sample presentations and sales tools. But scripting the entire call is ineffective, because it doesn't leave room for salespeople to tailor their approach.

If you're in marketing and your head is spinning right now at the thought of letting your salespeople loose without a prescripted message, consider some of the findings from our field study:

- Average salespeople repeat the marketing messages exactly as they have been instructed, using the same messages on call after call.
- Top-performing NSP reps customize marketing messages to help individual customers meet their goals.

- Average reps lead with a marketing message to get customer interest.
- NSP reps begin their calls by discussing specific customer issues and then weave in only those marketing messages that apply to that individual customer's situation.

- Average salespeople spend the majority of their customer face time delivering marketing messages.
- NSP reps spend most of their sales calls discussing customer issues. That's why their calls last longer and their customers are more engaged.

Another interesting study finding in organizations that were more marketing driven (such as pharmaceutical and consumer products) was that top-performing NSP reps often perceived that they were making an intentional decision to depart from the company prescribed sales call model by not leading with marketing messages. What's ironic is that these were the top performers, who drove the most business and had the deepest relationships with their customers.

One particularly exceptional NSP salesperson who was extremely skillful at personalizing messages for individual customers said, "I'm not going to act like some sales monkey who does a scripted show. I have close relationships with these people, and it would be totally inappropriate."

Trying to turn your sales calls into commercials decreases the close rate and erodes customer trust. It also diminishes morale and drives away top sales talent, because NSP-driven salespeople get bored repeating generic messages. Eventually, they look for more of a challenge.

Marketing and sales are two different functions. Although they need to support each other, employees in each need to understand that they play very distinct different roles.

Mistake #2: Failing to Flip the Switch in the Marketing-to-Sales Handoff

There's a point in every sales cycle when you need to switch from marketing to sales mode. The two disciplines require different mindsets and behaviors. In business-to-consumer (B2C) sales, the handoff happens late in the sales cycle, whereas in business-to-business (B2B) sales, it tends to happen earlier.

Organizations that sell to consumers (such as packaged goods, airlines, and hotels) drive demand through marketing. Sales provides a lift at the end of the sales cycle once the consumer is interested. The handoff between marketing and sales comes later (Figure 12.1).

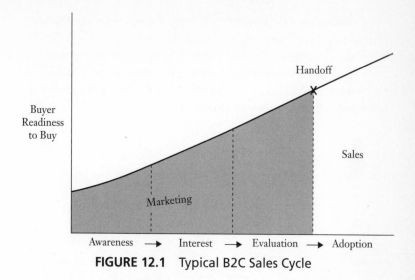

FIGURE 12.1 Typical B2C Sales Cycle

Organizations in a B2B environment tend to be more sales driven. Marketing creates brand awareness and may generate leads, but the handoff comes much earlier. As such, salespeople are responsible for driving most of the revenue (Figure 12.2).

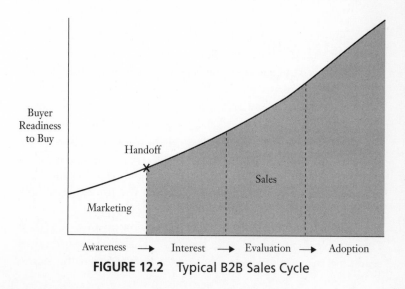

FIGURE 12.2 Typical B2B Sales Cycle

Businesses that are both B2C and B2B—consumer products, electronics, hospitality, pharmaceuticals, and others—rely heavily on both marketing and sales. Marketing drives consumer demand, but sales has to close the deal with the business customer, who may be a retailer, influencer, prescriber, or recommender. Both tracks are happening simultaneously, as shown in Figure 12.3.

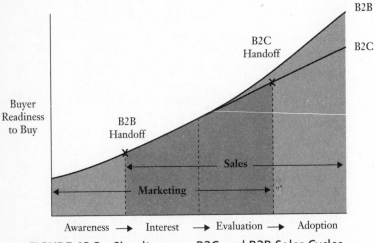

FIGURE 12.3 Simultaneous B2C and B2B Sales Cycles

Apple provides a great example of the marketing-to-sales hand-off in both the B2C world and B2B world.

Apple drives consumer demand with great marketing. People buy products directly off the Web without using a salesperson. Consumers who do buy from the store are likely already 80 to 100 percent sold on the brand and products by the time they reach the store. The store's salespeople provide extra lift and are very skilled at treating customers as individuals. They've been trained to ask about your life and work to make sure they sell you the right products. The Apple retail teams with whom I've worked learn how to tailor the sales approach to multiple customer types.

Columnist David Segal wrote the following in a *New York Times* article about Apple's sales training: "The phrase that trainees hear time and again, which echoes once they arrive at the stores, is 'enriching people's lives.' The idea is to instill in employees the notion that they are doing something far grander than just selling or fixing products. If there is a secret to Apple's sauce, this is it: the company ennobles employees. It understands that a lot of people will forgo money if they have a sense of higher purpose."

Apple's marketing drives the majority of demand on the consumer side; most salespeople are there at the end to provide that push that closes the deal. However, the marketing-to-sales ratios reverse on Apple's business sales side. Apple isn't the market leader in business machines (with the exception of a few industries, such as film, dental, and advertising). Marketing may create awareness, but many business customers aren't even 20 percent sold before they speak to a salesperson. Apple's salespeople on the business side have to be much more proactive about understanding their customers. When you're dealing with a business customer who is purchasing a product for multiple users, the sales are bigger—and more decision makers are involved. It varies by market and product, but in many cases, 80 percent of the lift has to come from the sales force.

Whether your company is B2C, B2B, or a combination, it's critical that everyone in your organization understand the point at which marketing stops and sales begins. Sales leaders need to know when it's time to flip the switch. A good litmus test is as follows: when you can't see or hear the customer, it's marketing. The moment you can see their face or hear their voice, it's time to stop marketing and start selling.

Organizations that don't know when to flip the switch have lower close rates, simply because they're still marketing when they should be selling. Their sales calls tend to be "visits" during which the salespeople repeat the same messages again and again. And you can't afford to pay salespeople for "visits" in a tough economy—nor would you want to in *any* economy.

Knowing when to make this shift improves your win rate, because it keeps you from wasting time on generic messaging. You know exactly when to change your behavior and your mindset as you move from the generic to the specific. You go from a push mode to a more collaborative one.

Mistake #3: Creating Marketing Messages for "Ideal" Customers Instead of Actual Customers

It's easy to lose sight of where you think your products and services fit within your customer's business or life. This is especially true for people who aren't out in the field regularly interacting with customers.

Shellie Sullivan, a former division manager for an international cosmetics firm, describes this scenario:

"I was in New York for a cross-functional team meeting, and we were having a conversation about why revenue was down. One of the marketing people said, 'I don't see why we can't charge $15 for a lipstick.' I remember thinking, 'You are not our customer. Our customers don't live in NY and pay $15 for lipstick. They live on highway 203 in Alabama and expect to pay $4.50 for lipstick.'"

The first thing Sullivan did when she became a division manager was to take a group of marketing people to West Virginia for a customer event. They were able to meet directly with customers and get an inside glimpse they couldn't get by staying in the home office. It was so successful that it became standard operating procedure across the country.

It's understandable that people who work in a corporate office might lose touch with a diverse customer base that may be scattered all over the globe. In Sullivan's situation, the organization's marketing team overestimated the customer's purchasing power. But it could have just as easily gone the other way.

Companies *under*estimate their customers as well.

This isn't just about knowing your customer's price point; it's about understanding the realities of your customers' world. Sales leaders have a better understanding of your customers than almost anyone in your organization.

In Chapter 9, we discussed the five critical categories of customer information: environment, goals, challenges, what success looks like, and what lack of success looks like. Share this information with your marketing team. Give them examples from individual customers.

In addition to helping them better understand individual customers' realities, it will also help them draw conclusions about collective customers.

Selling with noble purpose is about making a difference to your customers. When you help your marketing team understand the nuances of your customers, they can do a better job of helping you actualize your NSP.

Mistake #4: Creating Marketing Materials That Don't Match the Sales Cycle

We've already discussed how NSP-driven salespeople (top performers) think about the customer first and the products second. Your sales collaterals should reflect this mindset by addressing the customer's issue first, then citing your product's bells and whistles.

Marketing expert Alex Goldfayn, chief executive officer of the Evangelist Marketing Institute, says that the mistake of most marketing literature is that "it's too technical; it all focuses on the features . . . doesn't involve the customers . . . it's marketing people, or worse engineers, sitting in a room guessing."

Goldfayn, who works with organizations such as Logitech, T-Mobile, and TiVo, says, "When you don't talk to your customers, you don't deeply understand what's relevant, interesting, valuable, or meaningful to them. You're just guessing from a conference room."

And merely guessing at what's important to customers results in infective sales aids.

Imagine that you want to create a leaflet for a new product. You're naturally tempted to put the product front and center and then list the features and benefits.

But you know by this point in the book that product-focused sales aids result in product-oriented sales calls. And by now, you're very much aware of the perils of a product-oriented sales call.

As much as you want to tout your product, you know it's more effective to create materials that address the customer's goals and challenges up front—and put the product technical specs afterward.

One of the best ways to do this is to use NSP stories. Stories about how you made a difference to similar clients are more interesting to any customer than your technical specs.

You should also make sure that your sales presentation templates follow a similar NSP format. I often work with the marketing teams to create presentation templates. We include placeholders at the front of the presentation for the customer's environment, goals, challenges, and success factors.

The middle part of the presentation is a transition spot for customer stories and a description about how the solution will make a difference to the customer getting the presentation, and the back half contains the product information. (See Part III for the NSP presentation template.)

This reinforces the mindset of customer first, product second—the mindset that differentiates top-performing NSP reps.

Take a look at your own literature and presentations. What do they say? Do you list lots of features and technical specs? Do they describe why you're wonderful in a generic sense? Or do your materials describe how you make a difference to your customers?

The most effective sales tools are organized around the impact you have on customers. Creating customer-focused materials usually requires that you have several presentations and sales aides, because different customers have different goals. Your presentations and sales aids need to cover a variety of situations.

For example, let's say that one of the ways you make a difference to customers is to help them improve efficiency. You'll want a sales aid that describes how you do it. But you might need different material for different customer types, because "improving efficiency" might look different for different customers.

The message is fairly simple, although sometimes hard to swallow: what works in marketing does not work in sales. Marketing focuses on a single message for many customers; a sale focuses on tailoring your message for each individual customer. You don't need hundreds of presentations, but limiting yourself to just one will have a damaging effect on sales calls. You'll wind up with product-focused sales calls. Instead of bringing your NSP to life, your salespeople will become walking company brochures.

In an ideal world, a sales force has a library of sales aids organized around the most critical customer goals and challenges. This enables salespeople to choose which presentation or tool to use based on what they know about the customer and information they uncover during their sales calls.

Marketing Can't Play Cyrano for Sales

In the classic seventeenth-century love story, Cyrano de Bergerac writes eloquent prose to help the handsome foot soldier Christian win his beloved Roxanne.

It's tempting in the race to win your customers' hearts and minds for marketing to want to play a similar role for sales. Savvy marketers whisper the magic NSP into the salesperson's ear, the salesperson parrots it for the customer, and magically, the deal is done and you walk off into the sunset with your customer.

If only it were that easy. Those who have read the Cyrano love story may recall that it didn't end well. Cyrano, Christian, and Roxanne all wound up dead. Scripted messaging cost them their lives.

If you want to woo an individual, you can't use a script. You have to use your own words. Salespeople who parrot marketing messages are like ineffective suitors repeating the same lines again and again. They never achieve more than mediocre results, because they never truly connect with the object of their heart's desire.

Great marketing organizations create compelling messages to attract a lot of customers. Great sales organizations tailor their message for every single individual customer. NSP salespeople move and flex accordingly.

If you want to sell with noble purpose, don't let your NSP become a tagline. Marketing can create fabulous materials that work for the masses. But you, the sales leader, are the one with the power to make the NSP come alive for each and every customer.

Do One Thing

Look at your existing marketing materials and determine whether they are product- or customer-oriented. If they emphasize product first, reverse the order.

13

Using Purpose to Eliminate Turf Wars and Silos

When people are financially invested they want a return. When people are emotionally invested they want to contribute.

—Simon Sinek

The two men glared at each other from opposite sides of the conference table, looking like mortal enemies—and in some ways, they were.

Steve, the younger of the two, had his hands perched on the arms of his chair, clenching his fingers on the edges as if he were ready to leap into battle. Bill looked like a war-weary solider at the age of 50. He'd been through this type of fight before, and he knew it wouldn't end well. He loosened his tie, let out a sigh, and leaned back in his chair, crossing his arms and looking over his glasses, as if daring Steve to speak first.

It worked. Steve took the bait.

"My team can't survive on this budget!" Steve shouted. "Are you trying to kill us?"

Bill looked at Steve with the dismissive disdain one might have for a chubby toddler stomping his feet for more cake. Steve was always whining about not getting enough. Didn't he understand?

Bill had bigger issues to contend with; he reported to the top. Steve's petty demands revealed what Bill had long suspected: Steve cared only about his own department. He wasn't seeing the big picture. He thought to himself, "He just doesn't get it."

How many times have you found yourself saying that about a colleague? He or she just *doesn't get it*. It's the ultimate corporate insult.

The case of Bill and Steve is based on an actual interchange between a chief financial officer (CFO), Bill, and a division sales manager, Steve. The point of contention was trade show budgets. Bill had cut the budget, and Steve, the sales manager, wanted it back.

Bill's argument was, "We need to hit the profit numbers, or we won't be in business next year."

Steve's counterargument was, "We need to be at these trade shows, or we won't have any customers next year."

Who's right? It's hard to say. They're both doing the very best they can to meet the goals they've been assigned. And therein lies the problem.

Business is filled with competing agendas. Salespeople have different goals than finance people. Marketing has different goals than sales. Human resources (HR) and manufacturing have their own set of objectives. The list goes on and on.

And, of course, everyone believes that his or her agenda is the most important. In a way each person is right; each personal agenda is the most important thing—to *that person*.

If you're in sales, you've no doubt experienced the frustration of having to convince an internal person that customers should be a top priority. But let's be honest; salespeople don't always know what kind of pressures our colleagues in finance, marketing, HR, and manufacturing face.

It used to be common to say, "We have a pendulum problem," meaning that a company swings back and forth between two approaches. Nowadays, business has become so complex that we've moved beyond the pendulum problem. Now, we have an everything problem.

People on one side of company don't understand what people on the other side of the company are doing. Groups pull back and forth against each other in a daily tug-of-war that's ineffective at best and destructive at worst. Whoever has the strongest voice wins. The result is rework, misalignment, and missed opportunities. Over time, you wind up with disengagement, silos, and turf wars. Without a common purpose, the whole company suffers.

Your Noble Sales Purpose (NSP) helps you solve this problem. It helps you manage the natural tension between competing agendas.

Earlier in the book, I introduced you to the McLeod 6-P model, a framework that can help you bring silos together and reframe interdepartmental battles (see Chapter 3, Figure 3.1).

The story of Bill and Steve fighting about budget is an all too common corporate occurrence. Bill, the CFO, was focused on his P—profit. He had to deliver the quarterly number. Steve, the sales manager, was focused on his P—promotion. He had to get new customers in the pipeline for next year.

Bill and Steve's conversation would have played out differently if they had an NSP. They would have still debated the trade show spending, but it wouldn't have become so personal. Instead, they could have used their NSP to remind themselves that they were both working toward the same thing.

Without one, however, departmental goals overshadow company goals. People naturally focus on the area they know best. But when you have NSP as your hub, internal debates take on a different tone.

In the case of Bill and Steve, Bill would still emphasize his P (profit) because that's what CFOs do. Steve would still emphasize his P (promotion) because that's what sales managers do. But if Bill and Steve begin to look at profit and promotion through the lens of their NSP, they're both looking in the same direction.

The 6-P model reframes these kinds of conversation. Looking through the lens of NSP doesn't change each person's expertise; it changes each person's perspective. The question is not, "Should we or should we not do trade shows?" The question now becomes, "How do the trade shows rank against other ways of accomplishing our NSP?"

Instead of arguing about a single line item, they're now both focused on the big picture: their NSP.

Framing the conversation through the lens of an NSP takes Bill and Steve in a new direction. It's more likely to ignite higher-level thinking, which will lead them to discuss a wider variety of options. They'll start asking questions such as, "How do our customers benefit from our attendance at trade shows? Perhaps there are different ways of doing the trade shows. What has the past payout on trade shows been? What impact do they have on new customers, existing customers, and prospects? How can we improve that? What can we do before and after the shows to maximize returns? Are there other promotional areas that would be more effective than trade shows?"

The fact that Bill and Steve have different perspectives is no longer a negative. It's now a positive, because both perspectives will be serving their NSP.

Bill is less likely to be frustrated with Steve, because Bill knows that promotion is a critical element in the mix. Steve is less likely to be angry with Bill, because he understands that Bill's financial controls are important. After all, you can't achieve your NSP without solid profit. Now, *they both get it.*

The 6-P model with NSP provides a common framework for making decisions. It helps you manage the natural tension between departments. It not only keeps the voice of the customer front and center but ensures that you have all the other areas covered as well. Battling things out with your peers isn't the real problem. People only fight because they care. Case in point, Intel CEO Andy Grove used *Constructive Confrontation* to create a culture where people were willing to battle it out on behalf of the greater good. Intel's explosive growth under Grove's leadership, from $4 billion to $169 billion in 10 years, proves that when employees aren't afraid to speak their mind, conflicting opinions produce better end results.

The 6-P model requires that your company set goals for profit, process, product, promotion, and people. It won't work if one is missing, because they all play a critical role. Improved clarity about how the various disciplines work together to support your NSP gives people a renewed appreciation for their colleagues' perspectives.

Think about it. Would you want to work for an organization that didn't have concrete profit and process goals? How successful would a company be without clear product, promotion, or people goals? Instead of being annoyed that their colleagues have a different lens on the organization, people learn to value and appreciate these various viewpoints. They don't take things so personally, because they know that they're all working toward the same thing.

How Silos Turn into Wars

The root cause of turf wars is rarely bad intentions. Most simply start as silos. Departments of well-intended people create goals and objectives that pertain to their area of expertise. They build out their department as best they can using the lens that they understand most fully: their own function. But what starts as a silo can turn into a battle when the people in one silo bump up against another group that has done the same thing.

For example, people in information technology (IT) create systems that meet the data requirements but that may not be in sync with the needs of customer service. The team in customer service establishes new procedures for managing customer problems but may not understand the implications for operations staff, and so forth.

It's easier to solve the silo problem before it becomes a turf war—and that's where your NSP can help. As a sales leader, you are a powerful voice within your organization, because you represent the customer. Compared with your peers from other departments, it's likely that you have the best understanding of the customer's world.

Your ability to bring the customer's voice to the front and center of the organization helps break down the barriers between silos. In the absence of an NSP, departmental goals take priority over company goals. People naturally place priority on the area they understand and where they're being held accountable. Other departments with different goals feel like threats.

Sales leaders who participate in cross-functional meetings can use the 6-P model to reframe the discussions. In most cases, people aren't overemphasizing their own areas because they want to ignore the customer. They just focus on the area they know best.

The 6-P model with your NSP at the center provides a reframe that pulls the customer front and center. It enables people to look at how their goals integrate into the larger whole.

Creative tension is a good thing for an organization. The 6-P model with your NSP at the center allows you to manage the tension in a way that serves your larger purpose. The five areas may pull against each other, but the NSP holds everything together. It keeps each of the other areas from getting too far out of line.

If you try to get IT to understand HR's goals or force the finance department to focus on marketing, it's unlikely that you will be able to break down the silos through goodwill alone. But bringing the customer's voice in gives you a common focal point. It prevents your organization from overemphasizing one area at the expense of others.

To put it more bluntly, you won't eliminate silos by telling people to be nice and cooperate. You eliminate silos by having a common purpose.

The Cost of Overemphasis

You read earlier in this book about what can happen when you overemphasize profit. But it can also be detrimental to overemphasize other areas.

Which areas have been overemphasized in your own organization?

Where do you have silos?

Do any of these ring true?

- Finance creates a new budgeting model, but no one uses the new forms or gets their numbers in on time.

- The IT department launches a new process, but employees work around it so that they can continue using the old system.

- Product development creates a flanker brand, but no one sells the new items to the customer.

- Promotions start with hype but don't gain traction because other employees view them as a distraction from the daily routine.

- The HR department creates an extensive curriculum, but business leaders don't want to take people out of the field for training.

When people don't understand how an initiative fits in with the bigger picture, they view it as irrelevant. The problem isn't conflicting agendas; the problem is lack of integration. In a healthy organization, you want people to have different agendas:

- You want the finance people to have rigorous controls for profit.

- You want manufacturing and operations focused on continual improvement of internal processes.

- You want research and development to dream up crazy new products.

- You want sales and marketing to push the envelope on promotion.

- You want HR to be passionate about people.

After all, these different departments exist in the first place because you have different tasks to complete and goals to achieve. When the goals in each area serve your NSP, they will take your organization to new heights.

But when one department dominates, the other areas are compromised.

The following examples are signs that your organization may be overemphasizing one area without regard to your NSP and setting you up for silos. When you look at the list, do you recognize any of these happening in your organization? Check the ones that apply. At the end of the list are suggestions for solving these problems.

Signs That You May Be Overemphasizing Profit

- Senior leadership has limited contact with customers.
- People try to game the comp plan.
- You discuss customers only as numbers.
- You never discuss customer goals in meetings.
- Meetings start and end with financial reports.
- You discuss stock price more than you discuss customers.
- People resent senior leaders.

Signs That You May Be Overemphasizing Process

- Teams get bogged down in minutia about efficiency at the expense of outcomes.
- Salespeople spend more time inside the office than outside the office.
- Tasks forces grow in number and size.
- Internal studies take precedent over customer feedback.
- You begin to use lots of acronyms.
- Morale declines.
- Internal metrics become more important than external metrics.
- Meetings get larger and the to-do lists get longer.
- You spend more time on reports that meeting with customers.
- Manufacturing doesn't meet with customers.
- Salespeople become skeptical of the home office.

Signs You May Be Overemphasizing Products

- Product development cycles take longer than the industry average.
- You're creating products with little customer input.
- Salespeople aren't excited about new products.
- Product launches don't focus on customer goals.

- Product updates don't include customer feedback.
- Your catalogue contains lots of products that have very small sales.
- New products divert from core competencies.

Signs You May Be Overemphasizing Promotion

- Salespeople give away margin to close the deal.
- You talk about industry leadership rather than customer impact.
- Beating the competition becomes more important than helping customers.
- You copy the competitor instead of innovating for customers.
- You attend the same trade shows every year with no benefit analysis.
- Your advertising mix never changes.
- You spend lots of time on social media with no tangible results.
- Your incentive plan pits salespeople against one another.
- Your sales meetings focus on targets instead of customers.

Signs You May Be Overemphasizing People
(Yes, this is possible.)

- You conduct training for the sake of checking boxes.
- Vacation schedules are a frequent topic of discussion.
- Employees develop an entitlement mentality.
- Development plans are written without business goals.
- People expect rewards for attending training programs.

If you spotted your company in these examples, here are some ways you can use the NSP and the 6-P framework to eliminate these problems.

To Bring the Customer's Voice into Internal Conversations:

- Post the 6-P model on the wall of your conference room.[1]
- Use NSP as a decision-making filter. Ask, "How will this help us actualize our NSP?"
- Tell NSP stories on a regular basis.
- Record customers sharing their stories and show the video at meetings.
- Make a regular practice of inviting customers to your internal meetings.
- Create "a day in the life of a customer experience" for your sales team and senior leaders.
- Ask your team to provide examples of how they're bringing your NSP to life.

To Avoid Overemphasizing Profit at the Expense of Customers:

- Make a practice of taking senior leaders, including the CFO, to meet your product's or service's users. (Most executives meet only with other executives; distinguish yourself by exposing your leadership to actual users.)
- Put your NSP in your annual report right beside your financials.
- Discuss your NSP at board meetings.
- Be as open as possible about executive comp plans. (Secrecy opens the door for greed.)
- Include your NSP at the top of your internal financial reports.
- Send thank-you letters to your customers who pay on time.

To Avoid Creating Process Improvement Silos:

- Take cross-departmental leaders to customer meetings.
- Get customer feedback before you make system changes.
- Pair your internal process team with their counterparts in the customer's world.

---

[1]Download a printable version at www.NobleSalesPurpose.com/tools.

To Avoid Creating Products That Don't Matter to Customers:

- Have product development teams spend a day in the life of your customers.
- List concrete ways products will impact the customer *before* you approve them.
- Include NSP (customer impact) stories in product launches.

To Avoid Engaging in Promotional Activities That Don't Positively Affect Customers:

- Create customer advisory groups, in person and/or virtual.
- Spend more time talking about customers than competitors.
- Choose customer events over industry events.

To Avoid Ineffective People Development:

- Announce your NSP at the start of every training meeting or session. Ask each person to identify how improving his or her skills will make a difference to customers.
- When you write development plans, include a clear link to how implementing the new skills or initiatives will affect the customer.
- Make NSP stories part of new hire training and executive onboarding.

The 6-P model with your NSP at the center helps people calm down about the minor things and get excited about the major things. When people know how they fit into the larger picture, it's easier to manage the natural tension between groups. Turf wars and silos dissipate.

Nobody feels proud of building a fiefdom; people would rather be part of something more meaningful. As a sales leader, you have the opportunity to remind the other departments of the impact they have on customers. Just as you want to make a difference with your life, so do they. Your colleagues want their work to matter just as much as you do.

People are desperate to be part of something bigger than themselves. When you give them something exciting to focus on, their passion will amaze you.

Do One Thing

Use the 6-P model in your next meeting. Make sure you have goals in every area.

CHAPTER

14

How to Keep Internal Projects from Sucking the Soul Out of Your Sales Force

Purpose is far more than the starting point of great companies, it is the centerline that guides institutions to greatness over time.

—Ralph W. Shrader
Chairman & Chief Executive Officer
Booz Allen Hamilton

How many times have you seen an organization adopt a rigorous process improvement, lean initiative, or accountability program that starts out with a bang but winds up as nothing more than a meaningless, draining exercise of going through the motions for senior leadership?

The goal may be to reduce inventory, improve turnaround time, or cut costs, but the process winds up stripping away all sense of meaning and purpose. The very reasons that prompted people to start the project are forgotten during the grind of getting it done. Everyone loses enthusiasm, and it becomes a "make work" exercise that they wait to finish.

It's not just a callous corporate stick mentality that causes us to lose sight of our purpose; we lose sight of purpose in lots of areas:

- We renovate our home to create a more inviting space but wind up fighting over carpet colors.

- We volunteer for a worthy cause because we want to make a difference but become easily frustrated with all the committee work.

- We plan a vacation to spend quality time with our family and find ourselves snarling at our kids by the end of it: "We're going to have fun as a family whether you like it or not!"

Can you relate?

It's human nature to get bogged down in the process and forget the purpose. We become so focused on *how* we do the task that we forget *why* we're doing the task.

In his book *The Answer to How Is Yes*, author Peter Block writes, "There is something in the persistent question How? that expresses each person's struggle between having confidence in their capacity to live a life of purpose and yielding to the daily demands of being practical."

Infusing the practical with a sense of noble purpose is a challenge for organizations and individuals alike. It's particularly difficult for major, multipronged lengthy projects.

You read in an earlier chapter about why profit in and of itself is not a purpose. It takes the focus away from customer, and it has a chilling effect on morale. Yet many organizations make the common mistake of positioning big projects in the service of a profit, rather than their Noble Sales Purpose (NSP).

When a company launches a major initiative whose end goal is improving profitability, it often gets a positive reception on the front end. But over time, it becomes a negative. Employees see through the empowering buzzwords, and the once-exciting initiative eventually becomes another grinding to-do.

How Six Sigma Stripped the Soul Out of a Sales Force

Rob, a former regional vice president of sales at a large manufacturing company, who asked to remain anonymous, describes his organization's Six Sigma implementation this way:

> It started with a big rah-rah session. The CEO said: "This is the culture of our company; everyone needs to be schooled in it. In all likelihood the next president of our company will be a Six Sigma black belt."
>
> He told us that, "This offers great tools that we can use to improve our business. It will help us cut costs, improve process, we'll identify the bottle necks."
>
> They started forming all these teams and committees and bringing in consultants to do all the training. One guy practically lived with us for a year. They did classroom training, and there were lots of videos you could watch on your own. They introduced all these acronyms and tools that you had to memorize. There were tons of meetings. Different people on the teams were tasked with going off and gathering data they would bring back for the head honchos.
>
> The meetings kept getting longer. More people got involved, and more senior management started coming in for report outs. But through it all, not a single person talked about the customers.
>
> Some people were very excited at the beginning, but as the process went on, most of the people were totally

overwhelmed because it sucked so much time away from doing your job.

You had dozens of different teams, at different facilities, all running around gathering data. A team would occasionally visit a customer facility, but not often.

People wound up slapping things together just for the purpose of the meetings; they didn't really care about the end result.

The whole thing had a terrible effect on morale, especially sales morale—because it was all about the process. The people and the customers became kind of secondary. People started saying things like, "All we do is go to meetings."

What went wrong? Six Sigma isn't a bad program; in fact, companies all over the world have achieved efficiencies through its methodology. And the preceding scenario isn't unique to Six Sigma. The same thing happens every day with other kinds of initiatives and process improvements.

The problem is that the project became the end rather than the means. Instead of discussing the impact it would have on customers, the focus was all on internal benefits.

Rob describes how they positioned the end game:

Senior leadership's goal was to get the stock price to $60.00. They talked in high-level management meetings about how we were all going to get rich if we get this done. They even talked about stock price at the general management club, with mid-level managers who didn't even have stock.

I remember one woman kept asking the same question, at every meeting. She'd raise her hand and say, "I don't understand how it will affect me if the stock goes up?"

Senior leadership would mumble something like, "It increases our position in the marketplace; we're able to attract new investors and attract capital more easily."

She'd try again. She wasn't rude or anything. You could tell that she sincerely wanted to know, "What is this going to do for me?"

The CEO [chief executive officer] said, "Well, you're working for a stronger company."

It got to be a joke. She'd ask at every meeting and get the same lame answers.

Their goal was to take the stock price from 37 to 60 in three years. What wound up happening was the reverse—the stock *fell*. The company made promises to Wall Street about how much cost they were going to take out of the system. When those cost savings didn't materialize, the stock fell—because we didn't meet expectations.

We had taken our eyes off our customers in the process. We never fully recovered from this.

Unfortunately, this situation is not unique. This company went wrong in several places.

The first of these is the obvious morale problem. Expecting the employees to be enthusiastic about working like dogs to raise stock price is like expecting pigs to be enthusiastic about helping the farmer get a better price on the bacon. The fact that the senior leaders thought their employees would be motivated to help them (the leaders) increase their stock options is sad, but not surprising.

But there also are some deeper issues. Even if the leaders shared the money—and every employee received a bonus for improving the stock price—it *still* would have a chilling effect on sales.

Imagine a salesperson telling a customer, "We're implementing a program to take costs out of the system so our stock price will go up."

That would hardly inspire more customer loyalty. If the customer has any response at all, it will be to ask the salesperson for a lower price.

Even if the company does pass the cost savings along to the customer, it's still not a very exciting conversation. Telling customers,

"We're taking costs out of the system so your net price will go down" doesn't differentiate you at all. It just tells the customers that the only thing we care about is price—which is *not* the message you want your salespeople to carry into sales calls.

Remember, the internal conversation will always become the external conversation. That's why you want to be very intentional about the way you position things.

Through the Lens of the Customer

Robert Peed, currently a sales leader at IBM, recalls an early experience with quality improvement when he was a sales executive at Control Data. He says, "The standard of the day was a 90 percent quality level. A new entrant came into the market, and they were delivering product that was 98 to 99 percent defect free. Our first response was denial. But when it became obvious that it was real, we had to make a quantum change in thinking if we wanted to remain competitive."

Control Data ultimately had to go all the way back to design to make the required changes. Peed says, "It took a long time, but we had to do it to meet the customer requirements." While the process was undoubtedly difficult, Control Data's customer focus paid off. They emerged as one of the few original equipment manufactures (OEMs) that could compete with the Japanese. They eventually became Seagate, a worldwide market leader. Peed says, "The whole industry eventually transformed, and the people who didn't adapt went out of business."

The customer-driven lesson wasn't lost on Peed. In his current position as an IBM business unit executive on the hardware side who sells million-dollar systems, Peed says, "In my work group, the people who manufacture and design the products I sell are more adaptive when they get in front of the customer." He continues, "Without the customer, it can become a classic they said, we said."

Peed says that the IBM internal people are much faster and more receptive to solving problems when they hear it directly from the customer. "If we do this finger-pointing thing and say my product is great, we're not successful," he says. "When we're in front of the customer, we tend to learn more. If you listen to the customer, there is no downside."

Connecting internal teams directly with customers is one of the reasons IBM continues to improve products and dominate the market.

Process improvement is never going to be a joy ride. But when you position it in the service of your NSP, you're more likely to keep people engaged. Even if they're not chomping at the bit to make improvements, at least they won't resent it.

Big projects and company-wide initiatives are always challenging. Keeping your NSP front and center reminds people of the end game. Here's how one of our clients, Capital G, used NSP to manage an 18-month project that their information technology (IT) department had launched.

You read about Capital G, the Bermuda family-owned bank whose NSP is "We help people achieve financial success," in Chapter 9. Their NSP values are:

We deliver value. We build trust. We act with integrity. We are a family.

In 2010, Cap G, as they're known in Bermuda, initiated a project to change their core banking system. Their current system wasn't adequate enough to support growth, and they also wanted to improve the customer experience. They had to decide how they wanted the system to work and write procedures for every single thing they did. As a result, the back-end IT work was tremendous. The 18-month initiative wound up involving almost every bank employee.

There were times when people were so frustrated that they wanted to scream. (If you've ever been part of an IT project, you probably know this feeling yourself.) The operations team spent entire weekends documenting procedures. It took many more months to get all the documentation accurate. The IT team and subject matter experts worked nights and weekends on test data. All the free pizza in the world couldn't make these events fun.

But despite a multitude of challenging tasks, long weekends, and inevitable problems, through it all, CEO Ian Truran kept bringing employees back to their NSP by reminding people, "We're doing this so that we can help our customers achieve financial success." Everyone in the bank was trained on the new system a month before it was slated to "go live." It would have been easy to just jump into the technical piece, but Cap G knew it was important to set the tone and view the process through the lens of their NSP.

We kicked off the training with a 2-minute video from Truran where he expressed his thanks to the team and described the impact the new system would have on the customer experience. He also talked about why a local bank was important to the Bermuda economy and how supporting each other as a family (one of their NSP values) would help them get through the change.

We restated the purpose during each individual session. Every bank employee was trained in the new systems over a three-week period. On "go live" weekend, Truran and the other executives came in to work alongside their teams. On "go live" Monday, the executives were out on the floor with customers. Capital G senior vice president of human resources Rebecca Pitman said, "We wanted to support the people on the floor, to let them know senior leadership cared enough to show up for the employees. We were there to help them with customers if there were glitches."

And there were a few glitches, including an unexpected power outage in the middle of the conversion and an all-night marathon of reentering data. But the team kept their cool *and* their focus on the customer through it all. The end result was a successful implementation, and a team that believes in one another.

When you compare Capital G's successful launch of a new system to similar launches in other much larger banks—banks that have experienced system shutdowns, employees venting at customers, and leaders pointing fingers—you can see what a difference it makes when the leaders are focused on the *purpose*. To put this into perspective, many of the people who work at Capital G are hourly employees who didn't have a financial incentive to make the program successful. They just wanted to do right by their customers. Having leaders who continually reminded them of their

NSP is what made the project successful—and compelled them to want to make it so.

Purpose as a Touchstone

Big projects can give you big wins. The best way to get and *keep* people engaged is to position projects in a way that lets everyone know that it's serving your NSP. When people know that they're doing it for the customer, they're more likely to give it their all.

Implementing a new system, shaving bits and pieces off your margins, or plowing through reports looking for errors may not be thrilling. However, it's part of the hard work that has to happen if you want to live by your NSP.

We all lose our sense of purpose from time to time. When life and work get hard, we find ourselves bogged down in the day to day. It's easy to feel overwhelmed when you're staring at a mountain of data, a looming deadline, or a mess you didn't cause.

It happens in all areas of our lives. There's not a parent or boss alive who hasn't forgotten his or her best intentions at times.

As a parent, I have to continually remind myself that all the challenging, difficult, and sometimes boring moments of parenthood are contributing to something bigger. My husband and I continually tell ourselves, "We're raising the future president of the United States and her secretary of state."

It may sound overreaching to some, but it's real to us. It doesn't mean our daughters actually have to become the leaders of the free world. It simply means that we, as parents, need to behave as though they might. That lofty purpose helps us bring our A game to the more mundane aspects of parenting.

The same strategy applies at work. The more you can remind yourself of your larger purpose—your NSP—the better you'll able to bring your A game to the challenging, difficult, and sometimes even boring moments at work.

The Pulitzer Prize winning poet Wallace Stevens wrote in "Reply to Papini": "The way through the world is more difficult than the way beyond it."

Your NSP is a tool to help you make your way through the difficult world of work. Use your NSP to invigorate the projects that will make a difference to your customers and to remind yourself that even the most mundane moments matter.

Do One Thing

Think about a looming process renovation project, identify the impact it will have on customers, and make this message the centerpiece of the project.

15

Reframe Your Team's Internal Talk Track with One Pivotal Behavior

Behavior is the mirror in which everyone shows their image.
—Johann Wolfgang von Goethe

Can a single behavior elevate an entire organization? It can—if it's the *right* behavior.

Here's how a simple 1-minute act helped an organization reinforce its purpose and outperform its competition by leaps and bounds.

I mentioned earlier in this book that I have a college-age daughter. My family and I were moving her into Boston University (BU) over Labor Day weekend. The four of us, mom, dad, college daughter and her younger sister, were standing on the street, looking befuddled at the campus map. At that moment, a friendly and official-looking gentleman approached us, asking, "Can I help you find something?"

He introduced himself as the dean of students. He asked where we were from, told us he was delighted to have us on campus, and pointed us in the right direction.

Keep in mind that this is a major university in the middle of a huge city with 4,500 freshmen moving in on the same day. Yet the dean himself personally approached us. And here's the kicker: it's not just because he's a friendly extrovert. It's their official campus policy.

Any staff member who sees someone looking at one of the big maps is expected to approach them and offer help. One staff member joked, "It's a fireable offense to walk by people at the map and not offer to help."

They don't view it as a punitive thing. That single behavior—help people when they're standing at the sign—is purposeful for the BU staff. It was emblematic of their organizational culture and how they perceive themselves. It reinforces BU's purpose of "Educating students to be reflective, resourceful individuals ready to live, adapt, and lead in an interconnected world."

Dean Kenneth Elmore, the gentleman who greeted my family at the sign, says, "We should never walk past [people who are] looking at a map or if they visibly look lost. I tell my staff that [this is an] opportunity to step up and see how you can help them. If I do see that you walked past them, because you have other things on your mind, we need to have a conversation and think about whether or not you should still work here."

Greeting people at the sign is more than just a nicety at BU; it reinforces their purpose.

The BU dean's office website says their aim is to "enhance the quality, character, and perspectives of our students." Elmore says, "We have this incredible privilege: we get to engage these young people . . . from all over the world . . . in thinking about their hopes and their dreams. If we can guide them a little bit, that's invaluable; that's our purpose."

It might sound like a lofty goal that applies only to nonprofits or academia, but choosing a pivotal Noble Sales Purpose (NSP) behavior is a simple yet incredibly effective model that any organization can implement.

For example, consider what would happen if an airline established the following company-wide policy for all employees: "If you walk by someone in the airport who looks lost, offer to help that person. It doesn't matter if you're a pilot, a baggage handler, or the chief executive officer (CEO); be proactive and offer to help."

How long would it take before customers started to view that airline differently from the competitors? How much more empathy would employees and executives have for weary travelers if they had more positive interactions with them *before* they started complaining? How would the employees treat their customers if they saw senior leadership consistently modeling helpfulness and patience?

Here's how I observed it playing out at BU: A staff member approaches the "customer" with a smile, offering to help. The customer responds positively. The whole thing takes about a minute, and the customer walks away happy.

But the customer isn't the only one who walks away from the encounter feeling great about the organization.

The staff member is able to successfully solve a simple problem quickly and be thanked for it. After doing this once or twice, it becomes self-reinforcing. Staff members start to see themselves as problem solvers and ambassadors for their "company." And you cannot overestimate the ripple effect this has on the organization's culture.

That single policy sends a message to everyone, both inside and outside the organization: "Our goal is to be helpful. We care about people, and we place a high priority on interpersonal interactions."

When employees of every level personally connect with customers, they empathize with them and carry that knowledge back to their job.

That single pivotal behavior—"help people at the sign"—ignites a process that makes customers and employees feel cared about and connected. Community forms quickly.

Elmore describes the impact it has on staff members: "They're a lot more present. They notice what happens around them a lot more [and] are more actively observant when they are out walking to get from one place to the next. They started to pick up pieces of paper. They have to be more present in their environment."

Think about how many times you and your people have been in either your own or your customers' environment without really being present. Elmore says, "It's hard to talk on your cell phone when you have to observe [the things around you]."

He continues, "We are in a kind of circumstance that's about relationships and people trusting us. We can't get our work done if we don't have good relationships and people don't trust us. Our greeting people tells them outwardly—you are worthy of our meaning and attention. It gives them a model for how they live their lives. They can be really good at what they do by having really good relationships with other people. It's a small thing that has a great deal of power."

We tend to believe that behavior follows attitude—and in many cases, it does. This book is about how mindset change can result in a behavior change. But one of the ways you can fast track the NSP mindset change is to choose a single behavior that reinforces it.

Changing the way you act will change the way you feel. It becomes self-reinforcing.

Eye Contact

Earlier in this book you read about Meridian Systems, a company that provides project management software for the construction industry. Meridian general manager Geene Alhady repeats the company's NSP—"We help people build a better world"—at the start of every meeting. The employees live their NSP values: We connect. We collaborate. We care.

When implementing their NSP, Meridian leaders chose one pivotal behavior to demonstrate their commitment. It was simple: we smile at and make eye contact with one another. And it's something that every single person in the company is expected to do. Whether walking down the hall or in a meeting—whether you're the VP of Sales or the receptionist—you smile and make eye contact if you see an employee or customer.

It's harder than it sounds, because you can't be distracted on your phone if you're expected to smile and make eye contact when you pass a coworker.

Alhady says, "Every industry is going through a reset. You cannot go after business with the same old tools. Your competitive differentiator is going to be your people and how they interact with the market."

Smiling and making eye contact with your coworkers is a small but significant internal behavior change that ignites larger changes in how Meridian approaches the market. When employees pay attention to each other inside the company, they learn to pay attention to customers outside the company. *Not* being distracted becomes the company standard inside and outside the organization.

Measuring Your Behavior

It's always challenging to attempt to measure attitudinal issues. BU's Dean Elmore, who lives in the world of academic metrics, says, "I am always looking to find metrics for the way human beings relate to each other. I am struggling to find little ways we can measure it."

But BU has found at least one measurement to use, and it's the same one that sales forces use: money. Elmore explains, "We saw an increase of 12 percent in the number of students who are participating in our annual giving. That says something about the total good experience they have here."

Measurements, of course, are helpful. But there's no need to make this any harder than it has to be. The concept is simple: choose one behavior that everyone in your company or team can do. If you pick the right one, you'll be aware of the fact that it's working right from the start.

Here's a way to think about it: our NSP is [insert NSP]; that's why we always [insert behavior].

For example, Meridian's Alhady says, "Our NSP is to help people build a better world; that's why we always make eye contact and smile at each other."

My company says, "Our NSP is to help organizations create passionate, purpose-driven sales forces; that's why we always ask the extra question."

Capital G Bank says, "Our NSP is to help people create financial success; that's why we always greet every customer with a smile."

Choosing Your Pivotal Behavior

Here are some guidelines regarding your pivotal NSP behavior:

- It should take less than a minute.
- Everyone in the company should be able to do it.
- You must hold each other accountable for it.
- There are no excuses for *not* doing it.

You can have the best product in the world, but the only way to evoke true passion is with people. When you make a proactive decision about how you relate to one another, your culture starts to shift.

You've probably heard the expression "act as if." If you aspire to something, act as if you're a person who has already achieved it. If you want to become an organization that makes a difference to customers, act as if you already do. Your NSP speaks to your aspirations for your customers. Choosing one pivotal behavior is a concrete way to prove that you're serious about it.

Do One Thing

Choose one pivotal behavior and hold everyone accountable for doing it all the time.

A Manager's Blueprint for Creating a Noble Sales Purpose-Inspired Team of True Believers

Once the stage is set, the presence of an outstanding leader is indispensable. Without him there will be no movement. In the hands of a man of action the mass movement ceases to be a refuge from the agonies and burdens of individual existence and becomes a means of self-realization for the ambitious.
—Eric Hoffer, *The True Believer*

Selling with noble purpose is not just a technique; it's a way of life.

Noble Sales Purpose (NSP) is different from other sales approaches. In many ways, it's easier to maintain because it's self-reinforcing. Customers respond positively, and it taps into your better instincts. But in other ways, NSP is more challenging because it requires a mindset shift that runs counter to the prevailing culture of most organizations.

In Part III we'll look at practical ways to infuse NSP mindset and skills into your daily operation. We'll address how to use NSP in sales meetings, ride-alongs, and interviews.

As a sales leader, you're the linchpin. You're the one who decides whether your team is just another average sales force or whether you're really going to make a difference in the lives of your customers. Leading a team of true believers is more challenging than running an average organization. It's also infinitely more rewarding and a hell of a lot more fun.

16

Lose the Boring Slides

Sales Meetings That Inspire Action

The tribe is hyper-aware of what's being celebrated, and when you celebrate those that are moving in the right direction, you create a powerful push in that direction.

—Seth Godin

Sales meetings represent a great opportunity to ignite your Noble Sales Purpose (NSP). Unfortunately, most organizations do just the opposite.

At a typical sales meeting the program is usually about sales results, new products, or announcements about the incentive program and other internal issues. What do all those things have in common? They're all about what's happening inside the organization, they're not about the impact that the sales force has on the customer.

Compare the conversation at your last sales meeting to what former Nike chief executive officer (CEO) Phil Knight did during a recent conference.[1]

Knight asked all the runners in the room to stand. Then he asked those who ran more than three times a week to stay standing. A good bit of the room sat down.

Looking out at the people left standing, Knight said, "We are for you."

"When you get up at 5 o'clock in the morning to go for a run," he continued, "even if it's cold and wet out, you go. And when you get to mile 4, we're the ones standing under the lamppost, out there in the cold and wet with you, cheering you on. We're the inner athlete. We're the inner champion."

How do you think the Nike people feel at that point? My God, I feel like Phil Knight wants to help *me* run a marathon. Even if you're not a runner, you know that Nike's work makes a difference. It matters.

Sales meetings are a chance to inspire your team and reinforce why your NSP matters. I've attended thousands of sales meetings and have witnessed countless mistakes. Following are among the most common mistakes organizations make:

- **Sales numbers are emphasized without sharing customer stories**. This is the biggest and most common error. Numbers without customer stories erode your NSP. A big rah-rah about sales numbers does not improve sales skills, nor does it build a tribe of true believers. It tells salespeople, "All we care about is cash."
- **Too many presentations are given by home office staff**. Everyone wants to get in front of the sales force. As the sales

---

[1]As described by Simon Sinek on his blog *Start with Why*. I highly recommend Sinek's book *Start With Why: How Great Leaders Inspire Everyone to Take Action.*

meeting draws closer, more groups demand time on the agenda. The result is an endless information dump that doesn't improve sales performance one bit. Save these for Web-based presentations before or after the meeting.

- **Speakers don't understand the sales reality.** If your speaker doesn't know what type of customers your sales force calls on or how you differentiate yourself, that person shouldn't be speaking at your meeting. Every presenter—internal or external—should know your NSP and market conditions.

- **The successes of only a few are celebrated.** Watching the same people pick up bonus checks year after year does not motivate the masses. Sales awards are great, but don't neglect people who made a difference to customers, even if they're not the top producers this year.

- **Products are introduced without customer context.** A lengthy presentation about product features that neglects to describe how the product or products impact customers does more harm than good. Present new products to the sales force the way you want them to present them to customers, with clear links to the customers' critical goals and challenges.

- **Team-building exercises that alienate people are used.** Imagine trying to hoist yourself over a rock-climbing wall if you're overweight. Now imagine having to do it in front of your boss. Unless you're the Navy Seals, team-building exercises that spotlight people's physical inadequacies have a chilling effect on morale. Stick to team building that emphasizes NSP skills such as communicating and connecting.

- **There is no opportunity for skills practice.** If, by the time your salespeople leave the meeting, they are expected to sell a new product or initiative, then they should practice doing it while they're in the meeting.

- **There is no opportunity for salespeople to interact with one another.** Sitting in a darkened room watching PowerPoint slides is like standing on a street corner watching a parade next to stranger; you might ooh and ahh over a fancy float, but you're not going to call each other up afterward to discuss float-building tips. Meaningful interaction builds shared commitment, trust, and confidence.

If the preceding list describes your last sales conference, here are five things you can do that will make your next meeting more effective:

1. **Tell NSP customer stories**. Imagine kicking off your national sales meeting with a dramatic story about how you made a difference to a customer. What does that tell your sales force? If it's a big meeting, it's worth bringing in an actual customer. If it's a small meeting, have a salesperson or senior leader do it. When a senior leader describes how you made a difference to a customer, it tells your sales force, "Our work matters."

2. **Celebrate the success of your sales force and your customers**. When you announce your sales figures, include how many customers you helped. Instead of saying, "We closed this many deals," say, "We helped this many customers." Instead of saying, "We generated this much revenue," say, "We drove this much revenue for our company, and we helped our customers drive this much revenue for their organizations."

3. **Emphasize NSP in sales awards**. When you give out sales awards, describe how the big sales affected the customers. Also, consider giving out NSP awards to the people who assisted, the home office staff, and those salespeople who missed the big prize but still delivered solid results.

4. **Introduce products in the context of customer goals**. Use the NSP model: customer goals first, then product features. Before you describe the product features, describe the customer goals and challenges that the product addresses.

5. **Give your sales force the chance to interact**. A structured activity like sharing your best win with your peers builds teamwork and morale. Golf is nice, but you'll improve shared commitment with an exercise that pulls NSP front and center.

Sales meetings are your chance to celebrate, teach, and reinforce what matters to your organization. When you focus on your NSP, you improve morale, camaraderie, and sales performance.

Do One Thing

Choose one thing from the preceding list to implement at your next meeting.

17

Inspiring the Many Instead of the Few

Adding Purpose to Your Incentive Programs

There are two things people want more than sex and money—recognition and praise.

—Mary Kay Ash

Have you ever had to sit through an awards dinner where you didn't win anything? You're supposed to clap and smile as you watch the rainmaker accept a prize while you, the lesser performer, are supposed to act like you're happy for him or her. It's agony.

There aren't many jobs where they publicly publish the performance reviews. But sales is one of them.

Sandi Parker, the vice president of sales for Medisafe Technologies, describes what it's like to be left out of the winner's circle: "It's not just failure, but public failure. It's horrible."

Parker, who for most of her career has always been a top sales award winner at organizations such as Kimberly-Clark and Safeskin, says, the few times when she wasn't a winner were "total disappointments." She says, "You know you're not going to be on stage. You're not going to get any recognition. You feel like all eyes are on you, and there's a big L on your chest. It's a highly competitive day and you hate to lose."

Reading Parker's description, one could argue that the agony of defeat is motivating for top performers.

In many ways it is. But there's a hidden downside.

Imagine you're a top performer; you're on track to deliver $2 million for the year. You'll make the bonus club and go on the incentive trip. But then, you lose a big account in October. Now you'll never make $2 million. Do you quit trying? Do you throw all your sales into next year?

If your only incentive is money, you'll likely give up on this year and start loading up next year.

But what if you knew that every sale mattered?

Parker says, "NSP can be the difference between a million and a million five. If I know my work matters, I don't quit selling when I realize I'm not going to make it to 2 million. I might not win the trip, but I can still make a difference to my customers."

Parker says that when you have a Noble Sales Purpose (NSP) you have something bigger than an incentive trip. She says, "NSP is a long-term perspective. Successful people don't deal in short term; they deal in long term."

Your incentive program will get a few people to the top level, but the rest of your team needs a sense of accomplishment too. Even the superstars have an off year. You want everyone to have an incentive to keep trying all year long if they're not going to get a big financial reward.

Salespeople want to make money. They also want to make a difference. It's important to remember this when thinking about awards. You can and should give awards for driving revenue. You can also add NSP to the mix. You'll further motivate the top performers, and you'll also motivate the people who aren't at the top this year.

Here are three ways to add NSP to your rewards and recognition program:

1. **Reward people based on sales results and customer results.** Does your organization improve customer efficiency? Do you help your customers sell more to their customers? How do you help your clients improve their organizations? Find a way to measure your customers' results and provide awards to salespeople who excel at getting the best results for customers.

2. **Give out NSP exemplar awards.** Did you have a rep sleep in his or her car, in the snow, like the Graham-White rep? Did one of your reps go in at 3 AM to meet with end users? Did your support staff stay late to help a customer get a product shipped on time? Did one of your salespeople do the right thing in a tough ethical dilemma? Look for ways to reward the people who actualize your NSP. Rewarding NSP behavior means that you'll start to see it more often.

3. **Bring in the top sales rep's best customer.** When a customer talks about how a top rep made a difference to his or her organization, it makes the sales award more meaningful for the recipient and it has a halo effect on everyone else. Watching the top rep get a bonus often inspires envy. Listening to the top rep's customer talk about how that person made a difference provides the team with an example they can follow. Your customer will benefit too. Your contact will appreciate the recognition, it will reinforce why your company cares more than your competition, and it will differentiate you in a powerful way.

Do One Thing

Choose one idea to add NSP to your rewards system.

CHAPTER

18

The Ultimate Litmus Test

Using Purpose in Interviews to Eliminate Nonperformers

A noble person attracts noble people and knows how to hold onto them.
—Johann Wolfgang von Goethe

Imagine you're interviewing for a sales management position in financial services. You have interviews with two companies. One company's website says, "We strive to be the preferred provider for our customers by offering a unique value-added solution."

The other company's website says, "Our Noble Sales Purpose is to help our clients find financial peace and freedom."

When you read the first company's statement, what springs to mind?

Probably nothing.

When you read the second company's statement, you're probably thinking about what financial peace and freedom look like. You're also probably thinking about that company's customers, who they are, and what pain they need solved. You're already starting to engage with the company, thinking about its customers, and you haven't had the interview yet.

Now imagine that you walk into the interview with the first company, the value-added solution company. The first question you ask is, "Tell me about your value-added services." You get a lengthy discussion about their services. You go to the second company. You ask, "How do you help your customers find financial peace and freedom?" What follows is a discussion about the impact they have on people's lives.

Which company would you rather work for?

Let's flip it and look at things from the interviewers' perspectives.

If you're an interviewer from the first company, the generic value-added solution company, you're going to have to tease out from the interviewee how that person will connect with customers. You'll ask standard questions about past experience. Without a Noble Sales Purpose (NSP), you're left to the traditional ways of evaluating people. And how many times has a person shown you his or her best face in an interview but then not lived up to that on the job?

If you're an interviewer from the second company, the NSP organization, you have a better filter. You have the opportunity to observe. When you start describing how you make a difference to customers, does the person light up and get excited? Does the candidate have ideas about your NSP, or does it fall flat with him or her? Top-quality performers who will go the extra mile for customers will get excited about your NSP. They'll immediately personalize it. Top-quality performers will have thought about it before they come for the interview.

An NSP serves as a litmus test in interviews. If a candidate doesn't get excited about your NSP in the interview, that tells you everything you need to know.

Do One Thing

Bring up your NSP in interviews. Pay careful attention to the candidate's response.

19

Using Noble Sales Purpose to Demonstrate Value in Proposals and Presentations

Presentations don't win, conversations win.

—Scott Jensen
Sales Executive, Deloitte

Your Noble Sales Purpose (NSP) acts as the anchor for presentations and proposals. (Most presentations are anchored by the company's products and services.) Your NSP keeps you from giving a boring, generic description of your products and solutions.

The model we teach people, which can be used everywhere from a 2-minute hallway conversation to a 30-slide PowerPoint deck for a buying committee, has three parts. Start with the critical customer information, link to the NSP, and then describe the details of your solution.

Here's how the process works:

In an earlier chapter you read about the five categories of critical customer information: environment, goals, challenges, what success looks like, and what lack of success looks like for this customer.

An NSP presentation begins with a summary of these five critical areas because they establish the context for your solution. In a hallway conversation you might touch on one or two key areas. In a more formal presentation, you'll want to summarize all five categories on a few slides.

After a succinct recap of the client's environment, goals, and challenges, followed by a brief description of what success and lack of success look like for the client, pause for agreement.

Once you have agreement about where the customer is today, the second part of the presentation is a concrete description about what the customer will look like in the future after implementing your solution.

This part is where you describe how you're going to actualize your NSP for this customer. Note that this is *not* a description of what your NSP is. This is a description of how you're going to help this particular customer realize it.

This is where you answer the question, "How will this customer be different as a result of doing business with us?"

For example, if your NSP is "We help people build a better world," you should describe in very concrete terms how you are going to help this customer build a better world in ways that are meaningful and measurable to that specific customer. This means that you have to have done your homework prior to the presentation.

This second part is also where you can insert one or two relevant NSP stories to illustrate how you've made a difference to similar customers with similar goals.

The third part of the presentation is where you describe the product's features, pricing, logistics, and next steps.

You'll notice that this process follows the customer first, product second methodology used by top-performing NSP reps. Here's the presentation flow in outline form:

1. Summarize critical customer information:
   - Environment
   - Goals
   - Challenges
   - What success looks like
   - What lack of success looks like
2. Describe how this customer will be different as a result of doing business with you:
   - Provide a concrete, measurable, and meaningful description of how you and your company will actualize your NSP for this individual customer.
   - Substantiate your NSP with stories from other similar customers.
3. Include the details and logistics:
   - Product features
   - Pricing
   - Logistics
   - Next steps

Written proposals can follow the same format. We often create templates (written and slides) for our clients and leave placeholders for the salesperson to fill in the specifics for each individual customer.

This serves several purposes:

- Salespeople are prompted to use NSP methodology.
- Salespeople can do presentations quickly and easily.
- Salespeople must uncover critical customer information to fill in the placeholders *before* they give presentations.

- Over time, salespeople gather better information during the fact-finding step, because they know they're going to have to summarize the information in their proposals and presentations.
- NSP presentations and storytelling become an organizational habit.

Organizations usually make one of two bad choices: they either provide generic templates, or they let the salespeople wing it. Neither of these actions is effective. To create a top-performing NSP sales force, you need a standard methodology and space for the salespeople to customize it for every customer.

Do One Thing

Use the outline in this chapter to create a presentation template for your organization.

Acronyms Are Not Enough

Breathing New Life into Sales Training

People tend to talk about products in the abstract, but when you make it about the customer, it becomes more impactful. It's more satisfying for the sales rep.

—Rick Russell
Executive Vice President and Chief Commercial Officer
Sunovion Pharmaceuticals

Earlier in the book you read The Dirty Little Secret About Sales Training, where you learned that well-intentioned sales training is often forgotten in the field because salespeople (and their managers) haven't made the Noble Sales Purpose (NSP) mindset shift required for the skills to stick.

Bad sales training can erode your NSP, but good sales training can reinforce it. Here's an example of what *not* to do, followed by an example of what you should do.

Several years ago, I was waiting outside a hotel conference room for a client who was the head of sales training for a major telecom firm. He was running a session for his team at the hotel. We were meeting during their lunch break.

While waiting for him, I happened to overhear another sales training session from the banquet room across the hall. It was a program for sales managers of car dealerships.

Here's what I overheard:

The sales trainer asked the sales managers, "How many times have you heard your salesperson say, 'But the customer wants . . . ?'"

The dealers all raised their hands.

The trainer went on, "That's what salespeople always say. But the customer wants this; the customer wants that" (said in a whiney voice to demonstrate just how annoying these requests were).

"You're probably tired of it, aren't you?" he asked the managers.

The sales managers nodded their heads in weary agreement. The trainer continued, "Now let me ask you, how many of you have kids?"

Most of the managers raised their hands.

The trainer asked, "How many of your kids like to wear Nikes?" The managers raised their hands again.

The trainer asked, "How much do those Nikes cost?" The managers answered: "$75.00," "$100," and so forth.

Winding up for the big finish, the trainer shouted to the group, "You know what customers want? Customers want to take your kids' Nikes, and it's your job to make sure they don't get them!"

I don't have many regrets in life, but I sincerely regret not staging a public intervention on that horrible sales trainer. It took everything I could not to burst into the room and declare, "On behalf of good salespeople everywhere, I hereby demand that you put a stop to this program."

As it was, my client and I got a good laugh, and it makes a great story about what not to do in sales training. I can only hope that at some point the automotive industry will wise up.

Here's how a company with an NSP approach to sales training improves the performance of its people.

When our client Sunovion Pharmaceuticals made the switch to NSP, the company already had a solid sales training program in place. Training included a selling skills model, a strategy course, extensive product training, and several coaching programs.

Sunovion's NSP is, "We bring health and hope to the lives of patients."

The company didn't need to change its training programs; it integrated their NSP into the existing programs to enhance them. Sunovion director of sales training Ellie Eckhoff, who first initiated the NSP process at Sunovion, says, "Our sales trainers use our NSP as the anchor for all of our programs and skills models." Sunovion also uses the five NSP mindsets you read about in Chapter as a mental foundation for the skill models.

Executive vice president and chief commercial officer Rick Russell says, "When we talk to doctors we want to dig into their needs. The doctors are there to serve the patient too. If you position your products in a way to help them help their patients, that's where the win comes in." Sunovion uses NSP stories in all their corporate events. Russell says, "It's infectious. When salespeople see or hear about the success a doctor is having with a patient, it gives them more conviction when they are in front of their customers."

Here are some of the techniques we've used with Sunovion and other clients to make sales training more effective:

- Create a 2-minute video from senior leadership announcing the NSP and telling stories to substantiate it. Use this to kick off every program, particularly new hire training.
- Infuse NSP into product training. Most programs focus on product features and facts, but Sunovion reps learn *how* the products help customers and caregivers help patients.

- Teach the five mindsets *before* teaching sales skill models. This reframes behaviors such as questioning and listening in the service of helping customers.

- Use your NSP as a touchstone during selling skills programs. Sunovion posts their NSP above the selling skills model, and every skill taught goes back to NSP.

- Include the NSP question, "How will this customer be different as a result of doing business with us?" in your coaching programs.

- Include your NSP and the NSP coaching question in your manager trip reports or ride-along forms.

- Provide managers with the "Selling with Noble Purpose" and "Coaching with Noble Purpose" White Papers (free to download at www.NobleSalesPurpose.com/tools).

Eckhoff posts signs in the training department proclaiming, "I love it here." She says, "Every day I tell myself and my two sons to go out and make life better for someone. Our NSP proves that our company does that."

Adding NSP to your sales training will make good programs even better.

Do One Thing

Pick one thing from the preceding list to bring your NSP into your next sales training program.

CHAPTER 21

The Most Critical 10 Minutes

Precall and Postcall Sales Coaching

I'm a coach, so I take the issue of control personally.

—Pat Summit
All time winningest coach in NCAA basketball

A manager's words echo in salespeople's heads when they're with customers. Too often managers send salespeople off with "Go get 'em, tiger" or "Let's close this deal."

You can do better. A little Noble Sales Purpose (NSP) coaching from you will have a big impact on your reps' performance.

Here are some field coaching techniques you can use with your reps to improve their performance with customers.

Before the Sales Call

Ideally you want to coach your reps well in advance of their critical sales calls. But the reality of the field is that you're often on the phone at 10 PM the night before a big call, or trying to squeeze in some coaching as you walk in the door. Here's how to handle the most common scenarios:

If You Have 10 Hours before the Sales Call:

- Ask the rep about the five critical categories of information.
- Share an NSP story from a similar customer.
- Ask the rep to put into writing, "How will this customer be different as a result of doing business with us?"

If You Have 10 Minutes before the Sales Call:

- Ask the NSP question, "How will this customer be different as a result of doing business with us?"
- If the rep doesn't know, provide one or two suggestions.

If You Have 10 Seconds before the Sales Call:

- Do the 10-second game changer activity with the rep.
- Breathe.
- Think.
  - This about our agenda and the customer's agenda.
  - We have a plan, and we're flexible.
- Feel.
  - Ignite positive emotions by thinking about something you love or your highest aspirations for this customer.

During the Sales Call

When you're on the sales call with a rep, resist the temptation to take over. Your goal as a coach is to prepare your players to succeed when you're not there.

Here are some ways you can add value. Make a plan with your rep in advance for you (the manager) to play one of these more minor parts of that call:

- Ask the customer about a strategic organizational goal. Customers are often more open with the boss and more likely to share top-level information.

- Tell an NSP story when the rep cues you. You've probably met with customers in other parts of the country or world; your stories have a high value.

- Handle a difficult obstacle that you and the rep have agreed on in advance. Have the rep cue you when he or she wants you to jump in.

- Share some of the positive things the rep has told you about the customer and his or her organization. No fawning; be authentic and thank the customer for the business.

After the Sales Call

When the call is complete, ask the rep to give an assessment first. Ask:

- What did you do well?
- What would you do differently next time?
- What do you think the customer's key goals and challenges are?
- What does success look like for this customer?
- What are your next steps?

After the rep gives you feedback, provide your own assessment. Then finish with the NSP question:

- How will this customer be different as a result of doing business with us?

This process keeps the rep focused on NSP for their next call with that customer. You've learned that the internal conversation becomes the external conversation. NSP coaching ensures that your salespeople internalize the NSP-driven mindset and the skills.

Do One Thing

Use the outline in this chapter the next time you make calls with a rep.

22

Using Your Noble Sales Purpose in Tough Negotiations

It's a huge mistake to think that people in purchasing don't care about anything other than price. When the salesperson brings NSP to the front and center of the conversation, you get a completely different reaction from the customer.

—Keith Kuchta,
Vice President of Sales,
Kimberly-Clark

In an earlier chapter you learned that as much as 93 percent of a customer's response was based on your mindset. This applies to negotiations as well.

I used to teach hardball negotiating skills, and what I've observed is that people who view negotiation skills as a technique to get what they want are not as effective as the people who truly believe there can be a win-win solution. Said another way, salespeople who merely *act* as if they want the other person to win aren't as successful as the salespeople who truly *want* the other person to win.

The challenge is that many customers have been trained in the hardball—I win–you lose—approach.

Here's what hardball negotiators will do. They'll start by eroding your value story. They'll make it all about price. They'll tell you that the additional services you provide, such as customer service, warranties, and so on, aren't needed. They'll tell you that they're of no value to them. They'll strip away everything except price.

Then after you've agreed to the lowest possible price, they'll try to build back in the things they previously said were of no value. They'll say things like, "I can't believe you aren't going to offer any service. What kind of company are you? Don't you support your products?"

Do not be lured into this. There are some buyers who care only about price, but in most cases, the aforementioned behaviors are just a tactic.

Many major purchasing organizations split the users from the purchasing people. The users are required to vet vendors to identify which ones meet the standards. After they identify all the vendors who can meet the specs, they turn it over to the purchasing department, who pits the vendors against each other so they can beat them up on price.

When someone says, your price is too high, that person usually means one of four things:

- I'm going to buy, but I want to see if I can get a lower price before I sign the deal.
- I'm not interested and have no intention of buying. Rather than giving you all the reasons, I'm going to use price because it's an easy and fast way to get a salesperson to go away.

- Your price is higher than your competition, and I don't see any difference—or at least not any difference I'm willing to pay for.
- I don't have the authority. I'm not the economic buyer, but I'm not going to tell you who is.

Your Noble Sales Purpose (NSP) can help you avoid these common traps. To be successful in negotiations you need two things:

1. An NSP mindset. Remember, customers are reading your internal dialogue. Holding good intentions for them starts you down the right track.
2. Clear substantiation of your NSP.

The time to substantiate your NSP isn't with purchasing; it's *before* the decision goes to purchasing. You have to make the case for your NSP when you're with the users. You must identify concrete ways that your solution adds a value that provides a return on the investment. These can't be vague things such as "Improve patient outcomes." It has to be substantial things, such as "Our product improves patient outcomes by 20 percent, which impacts turnaround time by 10 percent, which improves reimbursement by 8 percent." You get the idea; it must be specific and concrete.

Ideally, your NSP substantiation is so strong that the end users are willing to put it in writing and take it forth to purchasing. Providing substantiation in writing enables the end users to demonstrate your value even when you're not there. It also increases the odds of success if your proposal has to be approved by multiple levels. The purchasing people don't typically pay attention to NSP claims from a salesperson, but they will pay attention to NSP substantiation when it comes from their end users, the people they work with day in and day out.

Salespeople who sell with noble purpose don't have to spend as much time in back-and-forth negotiations. When you're focused on making a difference to customers, sales are less likely to come down to price. Price is always going to be a component of sales, but it's just that—a component.

Bringing NSP to the front and center of every conversation reduces the importance of price and elevates the value you bring to customers.

Do One Thing

Substantiate your NSP in writing before your next negotiation.

Conclusion

How to Use Purpose to Make the Rest of Your Life More Meaningful

Regret for the things we did can be tempered over time; it is regret for things we did not do that is inconsolable.

—Sydney J. Harris

Earlier in this book you read about the two big human needs: connection and meaning. These don't just apply to work; they apply to everything. I didn't always know this, at least not consciously. For the first 29 years of my life, I was focused on achievement.

I had what I now refer to as a *check the box* life.

Go to college; check. Get good grades; check. Get a good job; check. Work hard to get promoted; check. Get married; check. Buy a house; check. Work harder for more promotions; check. I always assumed that if you checked all the boxes, you would eventually be happy.

I was wrong.

I did all the things in life you were *supposed* to do, I checked all the boxes, but I wasn't any happier in my 20s than I had been in my teens. But then, in my late 20s, I got a hard reset, a very hard reset: When I was 29 years old and seven months pregnant with my first child, I lost my 53-year-old mother to breast cancer.

We all experience wake-up moments—that instant in time when you quit going through the motions and actually think about your life and what it all really means. Like many people who have lost a parent, I experienced a wake-up moment at my mother's funeral.

We hadn't had a perfect relationship. We'd had falling-outs over the years, but during her illness we were able to put that behind us and become close again.

Cancer does that.

Now at her funeral, I listened to what people had to say about my mom. My mother was a teacher. Several former students talked about how her love for math and science had inspired them to choose careers in medicine and biology. Neighbors talked about how she had rallied the community to put in parks and bike trails. My parents took in two foster children after my brother and I left home. A letter was read from the mother who eventually adopted the two girls. She said the time they spent with our family was a turning point in their lives.

As I listened to people pay tribute to my mother, I thought long and hard about what a difference she made. She wasn't perfect, far from it, yet she had obviously played a major role in the lives of everyone there.

That day was a wake-up call. My mother had died, and I suddenly realized the obvious: one day so would I. My fancy house, impressive job, and even the great Christmas party I threw every year didn't seem quite so wonderful as I sat there listening to everyone eulogize a mother, teacher, and friend.

My mother's funeral was a turning point for me. I realized that while I had been trying to check all the boxes, I hadn't been fully emotionally engaged in any of it. That experience launched me on a quest to bring more purpose and meaning into my work and my life.

As I look back on that service, I suspect my mother would have been surprised by it. To her, life probably seemed like an endless to-do list, and she could never seem to get all her boxes checked either. I suspect that my mom, like many of us, found herself so busy going through the motions of life that she forgot to enjoy it. One of my biggest regrets is that I don't think my mother ever realized just how much her life mattered.

If I had the chance to go back into my mother's life, I'd tell her. I'd point out all the ways that her work and her life mattered. I'd let her know that she'd made a difference: to her family, to her profession, to her community, and ultimately, to the world.

My mother did some pretty important things with her life. If she didn't know it while she was alive, I hope she does now.

In many ways, my mom was no different than any of us. She was a human being doing the best she could in the circumstances she'd been given, hoping that in the grand scheme of the universe her life counted for something.

I've come to recognize that much of the unhappiness, anger, and angst in the world is caused by a lack of purpose. We *all* want to be part of something bigger than ourselves. We *all* want to know that we matter. We try to divert ourselves with pleasure or by building a giant bank account or by doing what I did, checking off all the boxes on our list called successful life. But at the end of the day, there is no substitute for purpose.

Since my mother's death, I've made a conscious effort to bring more purpose and meaning into my own life and to help others do the same. I make a point to do for friends and colleagues what I wish I had done for my mom—remind them that they make a difference and point out just how much their work and life matter, especially when things get hard. The lens of noble purpose has helped me be a better friend, spouse, and parent, and it's also contributed to my professional success.

But I'll be honest. For many years it was easier for me to talk about purpose and meaning in individual conversations and speeches than it was to put it out there as a structured business tool. In individual conversations, and in my public speaking programs, I had no problem talking about connection and meaning and making a difference. But there was always a little part of me that held back. I knew that people responded on an individual level, but I wasn't completely confident about putting it forth at an organizational level.

It was another lesson I had to learn the hard way.

Earlier in the book you read about the sign manufacturing company that my husband and I purchased, lost a ton of money on, and then closed. I don't regret buying the business because I learned a lot. But I do regret not bringing purpose into the company from the start.

When we first bought the sign company, we didn't plan for me to be active in daily operations. I would help train the salespeople, but beyond that, my involvement would be minimal.

But when we started losing money, it became apparent that Bob needed help. I began working with the sales and operations teams, I created marketing materials and launched a prospecting program. Our kids even answered the phone and did mailings.

But things still weren't working. We'd overpaid for the company. We had tons of debt. With the economy tanking, the sales weren't there to support the debt and operation.

One Sunday night, almost two years in, when things at the sign company were close to rock bottom, I had a speaking engagement with a local entrepreneur group. It was the group's year-end holiday celebration. As part of the program the members shared success stories. Two women stood up and shared a story that reframed my perspective:

"For two years it's been our dream to open a day spa," they said. "We've had setbacks on financing, we've had two locations fall through, but after much work, last week our dream came true."

They began to get emotional as they described what happened, "Last week, the men came to put up our sign." By this point they were wiping tears from their eyes, as one described the scene: "As we watched the crane lift the sign into place, we started hugging each other." Her voice now breaking, she said, "It wasn't a dream anymore. It was real!"

Every single person in the room could envision those two businesswomen standing there crying and hugging each other as the crane hoisted their sign into the air. In that moment I realized that our company wasn't some crummy little sign manufacturing business. We were part of the American dream! The day a businessperson's sign goes up is one of the biggest days in that person's life. All of a sudden our work had meaning. I raced home to tell Bob.

By this point we were out of money, our equipment was breaking down left and right, and Bob was exhausted from the stress. He looked at me like I was a bit crazy when I started spewing the story.

But when I asked if I could speak to his team the next morning at their Monday 7 AM huddle, he said yes.

So at 7 AM in a cold manufacturing facility, I told 20 rough and tough manufacturing guys the story about the two ladies opening the day spa. I got teary-eyed as I described them crying and hugging each other. I told the team, "We're part of the biggest day in someone's life. We don't just make signs; *we validate people's dreams!*"

There was dead silence. All the guys looked at the floor. I thought, "Oh great, they're probably thinking, 'As if things aren't bad enough. We're on the verge of closing, and now we have to listen to the boss's nutty wife talk about some emotional mumbo jumbo.'" Bob shifted uncomfortably and gave me one of those forced smiles you give your kid when they trip going up on stage or come in last in a race.

Finally the foreman spoke. He said, "You know, when we put up that Rita's frozen custard sign last week, her whole family came out to watch." One of the install guys said, "When we put up that new Dairy Queen sign, the manager asked me to take his picture beside it." Within moments everyone was telling a story.

I watched their faces light up. One minute they were blue-collar guys punching a clock for a failing company. The next minute they were men who made people's dreams come true. When the office staff came in an hour later, we shared the stories with them. They got similarly excited.

So with no money in the bank, looming debt, and a pile of broken-down equipment, we decided that we would give the business a purpose. We became the company that validated people's dreams. Every time we got an order, the salesperson told the manufacturing team the backstory about the business that had bought the sign. We started calling jobs by the name of the owner or manager. Instead of saying, "We're making a Dairy Queen sign," the guys started saying, "We're making a sign for Bill, who just bought a Dairy Queen."

When the manufacturing team finished a sign, they all signed the inside of it before it went out. The install guys took pictures of the sign with the proud owners. We sent a copy to the customer and put another copy up next to the front door so that all the employees could see the owners beaming next to their sign.

Bob and the salesmen started introducing themselves as "the guys who validate dreams." Within a month it was a different organization. People noticed; we started getting a little more business. The transformation inside the organization was amazing. I watched rough and tough guys who said they had never felt passionate about their jobs come to work on fire. One of the guys said, "I've been making signs for 20 years. I've never worked at a place like this before; this is different. This is fun." Keep in mind these were hourly workers who knew that their company was on the brink of closing and that their entire industry was in the toilet. Yet for the first time in many of their lives, they were excited about work.

One of the moments I remember most was a rainy New Year's Eve when the guys worked late. Circuit City was closing, and we had gotten the contract to take down all the signs, as long as we could have it done by December 31. The team had lost two days of work due to thunder and lightning. They knew next week's payroll was dependent on us billing the job. So without any prompting from us, they decided to work on December 31. They didn't even clock in; they just loaded up the truck and headed out to get it done.

And this is how it came to pass that Bob and I and our two daughters spent New Year's Eve 2008 in a Circuit City parking lot, in the rain, cheering the guys on as they wrenched huge neon letters off the side of the building. C—Yay! I—Yay! R—Go, team, go! C . . .

You'd think it would have been awful. But it wasn't. In fact, I consider it one of the high points of my career—because out in the rain in that Circuit City parking lot, I saw what's possible. We had created a team of people who knew their work mattered. They were true believers. They cared about one another, they cared about their company, and they cared about their customers.

It would be great if this story had a happy ending. But you already know that it doesn't. The goodwill and enthusiasm we built weren't enough to overcome a mountain of debt and a stalled economy. The company closed. We helped the guys find other jobs. We're still in touch with many of them. Several of them have told us that although they're grateful to have work, "It's not the same."

So why am I telling you this?

Because we made a mistake, a mistake that I want to help you avoid. We waited too long. I didn't bring purpose into the equation at the beginning because I didn't think a bunch of blue-collar guys would go for it. I was wrong.

I made the same mistake that a lot of people do. I knew what was in *my* heart, but I underestimated what was in everyone else's. Whenever I talk about noble purpose, someone inevitably comes up to me afterward and says, "I love this, but my company will never go for it." That person then proceeds to explain why his or her money-driven boss doesn't care about "stuff" like this, or the person will say, "The people in my company are too intellectual—or educated, or uneducated, or power hungry, or disengaged—to get into this."

All I can say is that my experience says differently. I've watched construction guys get misty-eyed when they put up a Dairy Queen sign. I've seen seemingly uncaring chief executive officers light up at the thought that their lives and their organizations could become something more meaningful than a balance sheet. And I've watched salespeople all over the world become passionate about jobs they once thought were only about the money.

The truth is, most of us hold ourselves back from becoming emotionally engaged. We want our lives to matter. But it's easier—and safer—to check off the tasks than it is to open our hearts and start talking about something big like purpose.

I made a mistake in not bringing purpose into our company earlier, just as I made a mistake in not telling my mother just how much her life mattered while she was still alive. I've tried to rectify those mistakes by bringing a sense of larger purpose into the relationships I care about and by helping companies bring more noble purpose into their organizations. Our current business was founded on noble purpose from day 1. Never again will I be embarrassed to talk about making a difference and doing work that matters.

My message to you is, DON'T WAIT.

Don't wait until your business is failing.

Don't wait until you lose someone you love.

Don't wait until you get comfortable enough to talk to your boss.

Don't wait until it's convenient, safe, or easy.

And above all, don't wait until you think everybody else is ready.

If you think your boss is cold-hearted, do it anyway. If you think your team will laugh at you, bring it up anyway.

Somebody has to start. You can be one of the people who holds back, waiting to see what everyone else is going to do. Or you can be one of the people who has the courage to step into a more powerful model of work and life.

At the end of the day, all we have is each other. Your life is a short imprint in the arc of the universe. The best any of us can do is leave the world a little better off than we found it.

When you create a team of true believers who do work that matters, you begin to change the trajectory of the human race. It sounds lofty, I know. But people who have a purpose do big things. They create happy families, they build successful communities, and they lift up everyone they touch.

The principles taught in this book will make a big difference to you and your sales force. They also work in every other area of your life. When you look at the world through the lens of noble purpose, your whole life takes on new color and meaning. You not only perform better, but you also enjoy things more.

But these ideas won't work if you don't apply them—right now. There are no guarantees in this world. You could have a long successful career and life. Or you could be like my mom, and your life could be a lot shorter than you planned.

So don't wait. You deserve to have purpose and meaning in this part of your life, the one you're living right now.

I told you at the start of this book that I wanted to help you learn to love your job. By now you probably realize that loving your job is a gateway to loving your life. When you restore the dignity and nobility to work, your job is no longer just a scramble for money; it's a chance to make a difference.

A life of noble purpose isn't necessarily an easier life, but it's ultimately a happier and more fulfilling one. Your life matters, probably more than you'll ever know. So don't wait until it's too late to appreciate it. Step into your noble purpose now while you have the chance.

Do work that makes you proud. You won't regret it for a minute.

Acknowledgments

It is with deep gratitude that I offer my heartfelt thanks to the people who helped bring this project to fruition.

First and foremost, the two men behind the scene who helped craft and shape this material:

The first man behind *Selling with Noble Purpose* is positioning expert Mark Levy, who waded through the clutter of my mind to help me bring my highest aspirations into sharp focus. You have done the remarkable, Mark. You looked at all the scattered pieces and plucked out the organizing theme. Not only did you help me create a compelling message, you connected me with a publisher, critiqued the proposal, and forced me—in your oh, so compelling way—to improve my writing. Your insistence that I be concrete and substantiate every claim took this book from average to extraordinary.

Hiring you was one of the smartest things I ever did for my business. You helped me bring my head and heart together in a way I would have been unable to do on my own. My income has increased, my clients are more successful, and my kids can describe what I do. If anyone reading this book right now is an aspiring thought leader, you're crazy if do not hire Mark Levy (www.LevyInnovation.com).

The other man behind this book is Bob McLeod, my husband and business partner, who did background research and handled daily operations so that I could write. You are truly a partner in every sense of the word. It is not a coincidence that our business has grown dramatically since you joined the company. People always ask me if it's "weird" working with your spouse. My answer is, I've always worked with my spouse; it just became more fun (and profitable) when we made it official. You're the best.

I would also like to thank:

My clients. I'm forever grateful that my job allows me to work with smart people who love their jobs and strive to make life better for their customers and colleagues. Special thanks to the clients whose stories, quotes, and examples added the color and context that brought *Selling with Noble Purpose* to life: Ian Truran, Rebecca Pitman, Nic Smale, and Lisa Siddle from Capital G; Jeff Connally, Melanie Fricke and the CMIT team, Scott Jensen and Stephanie Newkirchen from Deloitte; Michel Koopman and the team from getAbstract; Terry Scalzo and the team from Intel; Rachel Barak from Google; Stewart Bruce and the team from Graham-White; Keith Kuchta from Kimberly-Clark; Geene Alhady and Anthony Mass from Meridian Systems; Alan Carson and Denise Leat from Orange County Courts; Dave Myers from Seneca Medical; and Rick Russell and Ellie Eckhoff from Sunovion Pharmaceuticals.

My mentors and advisors in business and life: Alan Weiss, one of greatest minds in consulting who taught me (among many other things) how to get out of my own way, move beyond my methodology (and ego), and take my business to the next level; Chad Barr, who is helping me create my digital "empire"; Chip Bell, a longtime mentor and friend whose advice (and boat tour) in the early stages of our business helped Bob and I immensely; Amanda Setili, a friend and advisor who never fails to articulate the truth; Bob Burg, a fellow do-gooder who astutely (and graciously) points out the potential problems while there's still time to fix them; Sandi Parker, a fellow road warrior whose heartfelt comments about incentive plans helped shape the chapter; Stephanie Melnick, a friend and consulting partner from whom I have learned much and whose huge work on a major project allowed me time to write; Mike Alvear, a BFF, hot yoga buddy, and Web/Amazon marketing guru whose prickly (and wickedly funny) pessimism brings out the best in others; Shellie Kirk, a BFF sweat buddy who came up with the "everything problem" and whose leadership insights, revealed on long walk/talks, have shaped my thinking; and Lisa Daily, a BFF whom I don't see nearly enough of and a fabulous editorial/life advisor who always finds the funny inside the boring and tragic moments of life.

The experts and advisors who provided valuable insight and information: Jim Stengel, a fellow Procter & Gamble alum whose analysis and expertise provided additional substantiation and whose insights about chief executive officers helped clarify both the problem and the solution; Steven Nevin Pyser, who provided excellent ethics expertise and commentary; Traver Gruen-Kennedy, a gracious man who is going to change the world and who knows much about sales and helping others succeed; Alex Goldfayn, a marketing expert who is willing to challenge conventional (and boring) thinking; Chris Meyer, my go-to customer relationship management expert who understands the realities of field sales; Robert Peed, who much to my delight (and the chagrin of others) enthusiastically engaged in a process improvement debate on a holiday weekend; and Jim Collins, whose work continues to have a profound influence on my career and life.

The team at John Wiley & Sons, Inc.: Matt Holt, who loved the concept from the start, saw the potential, and moved faster than I've ever seen a publisher move in my entire life—10 months from our first conversation to a hardcover book in the window of Barnes & Noble on 5th Avenue is lightning speed—and your team ensured that we did it without compromising quality; Lauren Murphy, who oversaw the project and kept me on track; Christine Moore and Susan Moran, who polished the content on tight timelines; and promoter Peter Knox and publicist Heather Condon, who jumped into the project quickly, pitching TV shows the morning after our first conversation.

I'm also appreciative of the previous editors and agents who helped me on this journey.

It might not be PC to thank a competing house for their help, but Marian Lizzi, John Duff, Shelia Curry-Oates, and Craig Burke at Perigee have gone the extra mile to support my work, and I would be remiss not to thank them, along with my former agents, Laurie Abkemeier and Laurie Harper.

And my family: my brother, Jim Earle; my sister, Leslie Earle Freymann; and my stepmother, Judy Earle, who have always supported my work and cheered me through many ups and downs. Thanks for being supportive when I had to go nose down on the keyboard.

My daughters, Elizabeth and Alex McLeod, excellent writers both, who also possess excellent BS detectors that have improved my work immensely. I often joke that you two are the future president of the United States and her secretary of state. (Your choice about who takes which job.) But for me, it's not really a joke. After you two came into my life, I knew you were destined for great things. Knowing I was raising future world leaders caused me to up my game, as a mother and as a citizen. It wasn't enough just to do a job; I wanted to do work that made the world a better place for you. I hope in a small way I have.

And last, my dad, Jay Earle, who showed me from an early age that work could be fun. While other dads were dragging in the door grumpy and weary, you came home from work excited, brimming with enthusiasm about your day. Other parents acted as though their jobs were drudgery, a "have to" thing they were forced to show up for every day. But for you, work was a thrill. It wasn't until years later that I realized everyone doesn't love their job.

I dedicated this book to my dad, because he gave me a unique gift: he set the expectation that work can, and should, be fun and that it should matter.

Growing up, my friends always said that my dad was "like a big kid." I think what they meant was that my dad brought an ear-to-ear grinning exuberance to everything he did. Whether it was "jumping out of the tree" (onto our 50-foot-long rope swing he hung in a huge elm), making stilts for the kids, doing another "Earle" home improvement project, or saving a failing bank, whatever he was doing, he was all in. At the age of 77, he and my stepmother flew to Boston for parents weekend at Boston University, taking Bob's and my place because we couldn't attend. His 18-year-old granddaughter said, "All my friends agree. Granddad wins the 'most enthusiastic parent' award."

When I first became a manager at the age of 24, my dad said, "Congratulations, you've just become the second most important person in your employees' lives." He explained, "Next to your spouse, your boss is one of the most important people in your life. Your boss has the power to make your life miserable or to make your life great."

It scared me to death at the time, because I knew he was right. Over the years, I find myself repeating my dad's words whenever I do leadership programs. Countless others have benefited from his wisdom. My dad taught me that to lead and work with other people is both a privilege and a responsibility. At the end of the day, we're either making life better for the people around us, or we're making it worse. My dad made life better for his team and his family. I hope you can do the same for yours. I hope we all can.

About the Author

Lisa Earle McLeod is a sales leadership consultant, best-selling author, and keynote speaker. Organizations such as Apple, Kimberly-Clark, and Pfizer hire her to help them create passionate, purpose-driven sales forces. Her offerings include executive coaching sessions, strategy workshops, and high-impact keynote speeches.

In 2011 the *Washington Post* named her book, *The Triangle of Truth*, a top five book for leaders. Her previous book, *Forget Perfect*, was featured on the *Today Show* and the *NBC Nightly News*. She writes leadership commentary for Forbes.com and has been quoted in major news outlets such as the *New York Times*, *Fortune*, and the *Wall Street Journal*.

On the more personal side, McLeod was voted most talkative in her senior class, and her 2007 humor essay collection, *Finding Grace When You Can't Even Find Clean Underwear*, was enthusiastically endorsed by Erma Bombeck's daughter, Betsy Bombeck.

McLeod established her own firm, McLeod & More, Inc., a sales leadership consultancy, in 1993. Prior to that, she served as a sales leader and coach at Procter & Gamble and vice president of business development at Vital Learning (formerly McGraw-Hill Training Systems).

Her first job was working at the Donut King in Arlington, Virginia, where, at the age of 14, she sold more than 700 glazed donuts in a single shift.

■ ■ ■

Comments or questions about *Selling with Noble Purpose?*

We'd love to hear from you: Lisa@SellingwithNoblePurpose .com.

If you're interested in having Lisa McLeod as a keynote speaker at your next sales meeting or event, contact Speaker@ LisaEarleMcLeod.com.

Would you like to buy autographed copies of *Selling with Noble Purpose* for your team? E-mail Books@LisaEarleMcLeod.com.

For more information, go to www.LisaEarleMcLeod.com.

Index

Berkeley College